A REFERENCE MANUAL
FOR HUMAN PERFORMANCE MEASUREMENT
IN THE FIELD OF PHYSICAL EDUCATION
AND SPORTS SCIENCES

A REFERENCE MANUAL
FOR HUMAN PERFORMANCE MEASUREMENT
IN THE FIELD OF PHYSICAL EDUCATION
AND SPORTS SCIENCES

Edited by

David A. Brodie

Mellen Studies in Education
Volume 26

The Edwin Mellen Press
Lewiston/Queenston/Lampeter

Library of Congress Cataloging-in-Publication Data

A reference manual for human performance measurement in the field of
physical education and sports sciences ; edited by David A. Brodie.
    p. cm. -- (Mellen studies in education ; v. 26)
    Includes bibliographical references.
    ISBN 0-7734-8788-3
    1. Physical fitness--Testing. 2. Athletic ability--Testing.
3. Anthropometry. 4. Kinesiology. I. Brodie, David A.
II. Series.
GV436.5.R44   1996
613.7--dc20
                                 95-47646
                                   CIP

This is volume 26 in the continuing series
Mellen Studies in Education
Volume 21 ISBN 0-7734-8788-3
MSE Series ISBN 0-88946-935-0

A CIP catalog record for this book is available from the British Library.

The Edwin Mellen Press
Box 450
Lewiston, New York
USA 14092-0450

The Edwin Mellen Press
Box 67
Queenston, Ontario
CANADA L0S 1L0

The Edwin Mellen Press, Ltd.
Lampeter, Dyfed, Wales
UNITED KINGDOM SA48 7DY

Printed in the United States of America

CONTENTS

Section C   **Page No.**

Anaerobic and Explosive Power

Section D

Aerobic Capacity

Section E

Local Muscular Endurance

INTRODUCTION

Purpose

This manual aims to provide a much-needed reference text to cover the precise measurement, including selected results, for a wide range of tests of human performance. The book is written for students and teachers of movement science, sports science, physical education, sports studies, health science and related disciplines. There is a need for the book because currently a single text covering these tests and results is not available.

It provides not only a clear description of procedures but for each test also gives specimen results which would otherwise need to be culled from the literature. This manual provides for all those interested in human performance an authoritative text against which any new data can be compared.

Scope

The manual covers a very wide selection of tests of human performance concentrating on those commonly cited in the literature. Thirty tests have been included within the areas of strength, speed, power, flexibility, muscular endurance, aerobic capacity, anaerobic power, motor skill/co-ordination, anthropometry, posture, lung function and fitness batteries.

Each test has been described in sufficient detail for the reader to repeat the procedure with precision. The reliability and validity of the test has been stated. The objective of each test, the age range the test is designed for, the equipment needed, the test procedure, the scoring method and other additional considerations have always been stated.

The results of at least one major study have been shown in the form of a figure for each test.

The results have been presented with age on the horizontal axis in each case for ease of reference. Each test has been fully referenced and any significant variable e.g. ethnicity) has been recorded.

Benefits

The reader has available a comprehensive manual which provides the base-line materials for personal work without recourse to a number of alternative sources. It provides graphs against which to compare values or to give an indication of expected results.

Unique features

The manual brings material to be found scattered throughout the literature into one text. It will have a consistency and clarity of style so the reader will know what to expect when reference is made to different tests. Each test has been reviewed in the literature using the Silver Platter CD-ROM retrieval system using either Sports Discus or Medline so is authoritative. It has a clear table or figure for each test giving results of the test by age group (if appropriate). This provides data for direct comparison by the reader. This text is not intended to provide a detailed critique of each test; it is essentially a working manual for students and staff to use on a regular basis.

The manual has been subdivided into eight sections which help orientate the reader to the test of interest. These sections are:

A	:	Kinanthropometry
B	:	Muscle function
C	:	Anaerobic and explosive power
D	:	Aerobic capacity
E	:	Local muscular endurance
F	:	Speed and agility
G	:	Test batteries
H	:	Others

Each of the 30 chapters has a place within one of the above sections as shown in the contents. Each chapter was produced by a student as part of the Integrated Issues module on the BSc (Hons) degree in Movement Science at the University of Liverpool. This manual has thus essentially been produced by a small group of students. This has the benefit that the students can empathise with the needs of other undergraduates. The responsibility of the editor has been to attempt a consistency of approach, to keep the text to a manageable size and to bring the manual from draft to reality.

I am confident that this manual will be a useful addition to the test and measurement literature and that it may be the basis for more productive activity in that area of study.

David A. Brodie
Editor
June, 1995

CHAPTER 1 : BODY MASS INDEX

Purpose of the test: To provide a general index of body fatness. Body mass index (BMI) is designed to describe the proportion of fat in relation to body mass regardless of height.

Common Usages: Body mass index is a useful way of classifying overweight and obesity. A BMI of greater than 40 indicates type III obesity (high risk), Grade II (or moderate risk obesity) is a BMI of 30-40; Grade I (or low risk obesity) is a BMI of 25-29.9; and Grade 0 which is the desirable range of body fatness is a BMI of 20-24.9.

Equipment: Stature measurement requires a vertical board with an attached metric rule and a horizontal headboard which can be brought into contact with the most superior point on the head. This is termed a "stadiometer". General agreement is that mass should be measured using a beam scale with moveable weights.

Procedure:

The subject's height should be measured without shoes, and to the nearest half centimetre. It has been suggested that standing with the back against a support helps the subject to stretch to his/her full height. The chin is tucked in slightly and the head held erect. The top of the stadiometer is used to form a right angle to the backboard, and is pressed firmly on the subject's head. Stature can also be measured using a fixed or moveable anthropometer. The subject should be weighed to the nearest 0.1 kg, wearing a minimum of clothing.

Special notes:

Also known as Quetelet's index. BMI is affected by 1) age, 2) sex, 3) ethnicity, 4) type of activity and 5) level of training.

Caution must be taken when comparing individuals with the normative data. Subjects with high body masses, but who are also lean and muscular have relatively high BMI values. The body fat proportions of such individuals when compared to normative data would be misleading. It assumes that only slight differences exist in lean body mass in subjects of identical height. Therefore the higher the BMI the greater the proportion of body fat. Because of this assumption, it is prudent to consider muscularity when high BMI observations are made in individuals.

It has been suggested that there is a positive

association between BMI and risk of major cardiovascular disease.

Validity and reliability: Face validity accepted. Reliability reported as high as 0.99 for height and 0.98 for mass.

Scoring: The score is the value obtained from mass (kg) divided by height^2 (m^2).

References: Andres R., Elahi D., Tobin J.D., Muller D.C., Brant L. Impact of age on weight goals. *Annals of Internal Medicine*, 103 (6), p1030-1033, 1985.

Tanner and Whitehouse. *Height and weight standard charts for boys and girls aged 0-19 years*. Castlemead Publications, (wall charts).

Figure 1.1 BMI standard chart for boys aged 0-19 years

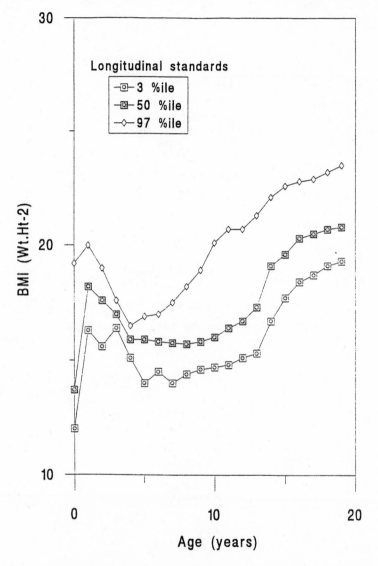

Source: Tanner & Whitehouse. Height and weight
standard charts for boys aged 0-19 years
(Castlemead Publications, chart No. GDB11A).

Figure 1.2 BMI standard chart for girls aged 0-19

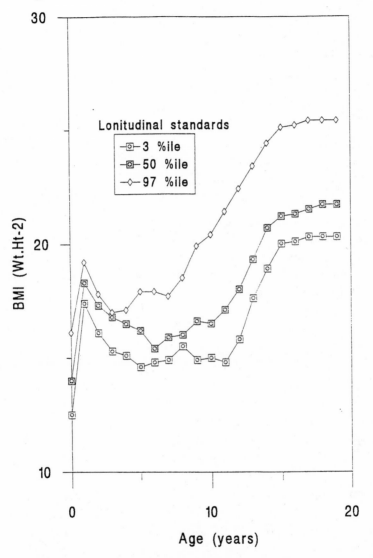

Source: Tanner and Whitehouse. Height and weight standard charts for girls aged 0-19 years (Castlemead Publications, chart No. GDG12A).

Figure 1.3 BMI standard chart
for adult male and females

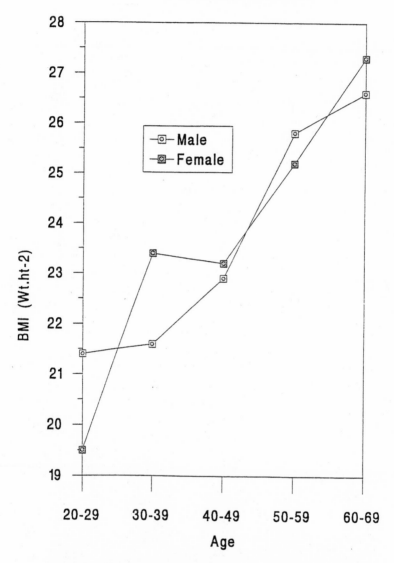

Source: Andres et al (1985). Impact of age on weight goals. Annals of Internal Medicine, 103, p1030-1033.

CHAPTER 2 : WAIST TO HIP RATIO

Purpose of the test: The waist to hip girth characterizes the different types of fat distribution. The ratio indicates the amount of fat deposited on the trunk, and reflects the ratio of the upper body obesity to lower body obesity. A high waist-to-hip ratio indicates the upper body or masculine type of obesity pattern and a greater risk of diseases such as non-insulin dependent diabetes mellitus; whereas a low ratio indicates lower body or female type obesity, and a decreased risk of diabetes mellitus.

Common Usages: Most results are presented for adults, since only after the onset of puberty does the waist to hip ratio seem to be an indicator of body fat distribution.

Equipment: Anthropometric tape for measurement of girths.

Procedure: Measurement of waist and hip circumferences should not be performed over clothing. If clothing must be worn then it should be only light underwear. Waist circumferences are measured to the nearest centimetre, at the smallest circumference of the torso, at the level of the natural waist. The subject stands erect, with the abdomen relaxed, arms by sides, feet together and breathing normally. Hip circumference is measured to the nearest centimetre at the greatest diameter of the gluteus muscles.

Special notes:

The waist-hip ratio is positively associated with adverse metabolic outcomes, elevated blood pressure, diabetes, myocardial infarction and stroke. An alternative (traditional) procedure is assessed through skinfold thickness measurements, measurements of girth circumference, and more recently computerized tomography and magnetic resonance imaging.

Waist circumference has usually been measured as the smallest circumference of the torso, at the level of the natural waist. However some texts measure at the level of the umbilicus, but this leads to recording larger values.

Validity and reliability:

Face validity accepted. Reliability reported as high as 0.98 for the hip circumference, 0.90 at the waist, and 0.92 for the waist-hip ratio.

Scoring:

Waist-hip ratio scores were calculated using the formula waist circumference (in cm) divided by hip circumference (in cm).

9

References:

Andres R., Elahi D., Tobin J.D., Muller D.C., Brant L. Impact of age on weight goals. *Annals of Internal Medicine*, 103 (6), p1030-1033, 1985.

Cox B.D. Body measurements (heights, weights, girths etc). The *Health and Lifestyle Survey*. Health Promotions Research Trust, London, p 35-41, 1987.

Figure 2.1 Waist-hip ratio standard chart

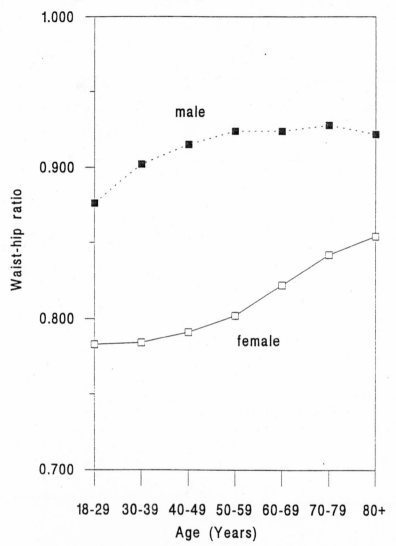

Age (Years)

Source: Cox (1987) The Health and Lifestyle Survey. Health Promotions Research Trust, London p35-41.

CHAPTER 3 : GONIOMETRY

Purpose of the test: To measure the range of motion of a joint in degrees.

Common usages: Male and female subjects. Can be administered from 6 years to maturity and beyond.

Equipment: Goniometer, obtainable from J. A. Preston Co. 71 Fifth Avenue, New York, NY 10003.

Procedure: Measurements have to be carried out on the nude skin. The tester palpates two specific anthropometric reference points for each segment. The joint being measured should be marked in felt-tip pen. The goniometer has to be positioned so that the arms coincide with the longitudinal axes of the moving segments in the end position of the movement. One arm is attached at the zero line of the protractor and the other arm is moveable.

Special notes: Can be used for all joints across the body and is inexpensive. Simple to use although a good knowledge of anatomical terms is necessary to carry out the measurements correctly. The goniometer needs to be calibrated regularly to give accurate readings. A general warm up prior to the main activity and prior to flexibility is advisable.

Validity and reliability: Face validity is acceptable. Test-retest reliability of 0.90 to 0.98. Intertester reliability of 0.25 to 0.91. Intratester reliability of 0.90.

Scoring: Range of motion is the difference between the joint angles (in degrees) measured at the extremes of the movement.

References: Einkauf K.D., Gohdes L.M., Jensen M.G., Jewell J.M. Changes in spinal mobility with increasing age in women. *Physical Therapy*, 67 (3), 370-375, 1987.

Gajdosik L.R., Bohannon W.R. Clinical measurement of range of motion review of goniometry emphasising reliability and validity. *Physical Therapy*, 67 (12), 1867-1871, 1987.

Heyward H.V. Second Edition *Advanced fitness assessment and exercise prescription* 218-220, Human Kinetics, Champaign, Illinois, 1991.

Figure 3.1: Flexibility norms for males and females

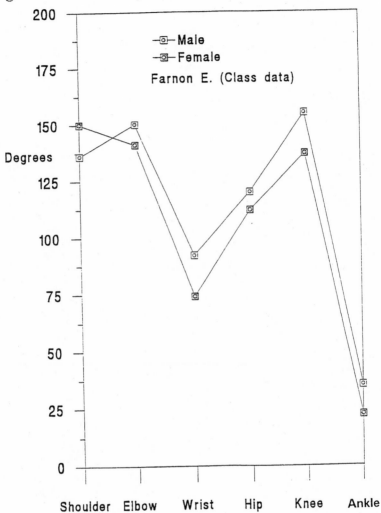

Flexion joint measurement

CHAPTER 4 : SCOLIOMETRY

Purpose: Used for non-invasive detection of scoliosis. Scoliosis is a pathological lateral curvature of the spine.

Common usages: Screening programmes of school children. Abnormalities can usually be detected by 10 years of age, although extreme scoliosis may be noted soon after birth. Those identified with problems in the initial screening process can be referred to a specialist for criterion testing, eg. Cobb Angle method using erect posterior-anterior radiograph. Specialists use the scoliometer to monitor alterations of pathological conditions with treatment, thus reducing exposure to radiation.

Equipment: The scoliometer (Orthopedic Systems, Inc., Hayward, California), is a specially designed inclinometer. A ball-bearing located within a fluid-filled U-tube indicates the angle of trunk inclination against a scale at the peak of lumbar and thoracic deformity.

Procedure: The standing subject assumes a forward-bending posture with the trunk approximately parallel with the floor and feet shoulder-width apart. The subject's arms are allowed to hang freely with palms resting lightly on the shins. The examiner places the scoliometer on the subject's back, with the centre of the device corresponding to the centre contour of the trunk, along the spinal column.

Starting where the neck joins the trunk, the scoliometer is run down the spine to the sacrum, the maximum values for thoracic and lumbar areas being recorded.

Validity and reliability: Intratester and intertester reliability of r=0.86-0.97 have been recorded. Comparison of the scoliometer with Cobb angle by radiography have recorded relationships of r=0.59-0.75.

Scoring: Scoliometer readings in excess of 5 degrees are taken to indicate significant scoliosis and should be referred to a general practitioner or scoliosis specialist for radiography examination.

Notes: The scoliometer is less sensitive for diagnosis of lumbar scoliosis, as lateral spinal curvature may occur without axial trunk rotation in this region. Lateral deviations are found most commonly in scoliosis. Non-structural scoliosis may be formed by disparity in leg-length and is non-progressive.

Structural scoliosis is more serious and liable to progress through the growth period.

The criterion method of assessing spinal curvature for scoliosis uses radiography. This method cannot be used to assess the posture of healthy subjects because of the risk of exposure to radiation.

References:

Amendt L.E., Ause-Ellias K.L., Eybers J.L., Wadsworth C.T., Nielson D.H. and Weinsteing S.L. (1990) Validity and reliability of the scoliometer. *Physical Therapy*, 70, (2), 108-117, 1990.

Lonstein J.E. Natural history and school screening for scoliosis. *Orthopedic Clinics of North America* 19, (2), 227-236, 1988.

McCarthy R.E. Prevention of the complications of scoliosis by early detection. *Clinical Orthopaedics and Related Research* 222,(Sept), 73-78, 1987.

Mittial R.L., Aggerval R., Sarwal A.K. School screening for scoliosis in India. *International Orthopaedics* 11, 335-338, 1987.

Figure 4.1   Incidence of significant scoliosis in various
school screening programmes

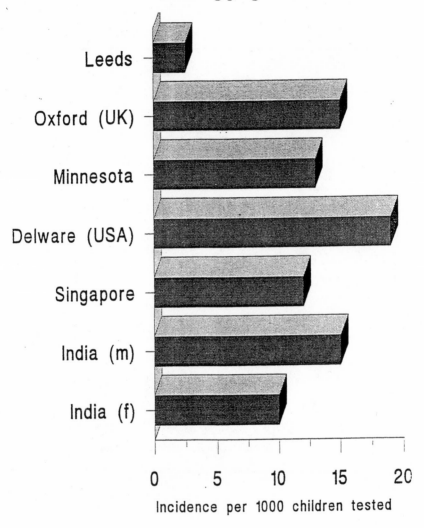

Incidence per 1000 children tested

CHAPTER 5 : KYPHOMETRY

Purpose: The measurement of sagittal spinal curvature, that is, lumbar lordosis and thoracic kyphosis.

Common usages: Looking at changes of curvature with age, injury or illness. Specialists may use the kyphometer to monitor alterations of pathological conditions with treatment, thus reducing exposure to radiation. As yet no screening programme of sagittal curvature has been reported.

Equipment: Debrunner's kyphometer (Proetek AG, Bern, Switzerland) measures the angle between two blocks, each of which span two spinal processes. The angles of the two blocks are transmitted via parallel struts to the protractor scale (accurate to 1°).

Procedure :   The subject is instructed to stand in an upright but relaxed posture, looking straight ahead, breathing normally with arms hanging loosely by the body. Shoulders should be relaxed and the subject should be barefoot with heels together.

In order to measure thoracic kyphosis, one block of the kyphometer is located over the first and second thoracic vertebra and the other over the eleventh and twelfth thoracic vertebra. The kyphosis angle is read directly from the kyphometer.

Lumbar curvature is measured between the eleventh and twelfth thoracic vertebra and the first and second sacral vertebra. The angle read directly from the kyphometer is lumbar lordosis.

Validity and Reliability: Reproducibility of kyphometer readings vary from $r=0.91-0.94$. Correlation with radiographs of $r=0.88-0.94$ have been reported, (Salisbury & Porter, 1987).

Notes: Erect spinal curvature is the basis of acceptable posture. Expert opinion differs as to what constitutes 'good' posture; a term relating to energy economy and cosmetic acceptability. Large variations can be seen in groups of healthy subjects. Significant individual variation can be seen between slumped/erect states and deep inhalation/exhalation. It is important, therefore to standardize the position for each subject as shown above. Spinal curvature also changes with age, due to reduction in elasticity of the spinal liagaments and changes in bone mineral content.

Both 'flat back' and excessive curvature are considered problematical, having an association with subsequent back pain.

Scoring :

Kyphosis of 20-45° and lordosis of 40-60° have been considered to indicate normal ranges, Roaf (1960). Fon *et al.* (1980) suggested that these figures are inappropriate for children and teenagers due to the changes in curvature during development (see Figure 5.1)

The criterion method of assessing spinal curvature for pathologies in the sagittal plane uses radiography. This method cannot be used for assessing the posture of healthy subjects because of the time, expense and risk of exposure to radiation.

References:

Fon G., Pitt M.J., Thies A.C. Thoracic kyphosis: Range in normal subjects. *American Journal of Roentgenology,* 124, 979-983, 1980.

Ohlen G., Spangfort E., Tingwall C. Measurement of spinal sagittal configuration and mobility with Debrunner's kyphometer. *Spine,* 14, (6), 580-583, 1989.

Roaf R. The basic anatomy of scoliosis. *Journal of Bone and Joint Surgery,* 48B, 40-59, 1960

Salisbury P.J., Porter R.W. Measurement of lumbar sagittal mobility: A comparison of methods. *Spine*, 12, 190-193, 1987.

Willner S., Johnsson B. Thoracic kyphosis and lumbar lordosis during the growth period in children. *Acta Paediatrica Scandinavica*, 72, 873-878, 1983.

Figure 5.1. Thoracic kyphosis during the growth period in children (Willner & Johnson 1983)

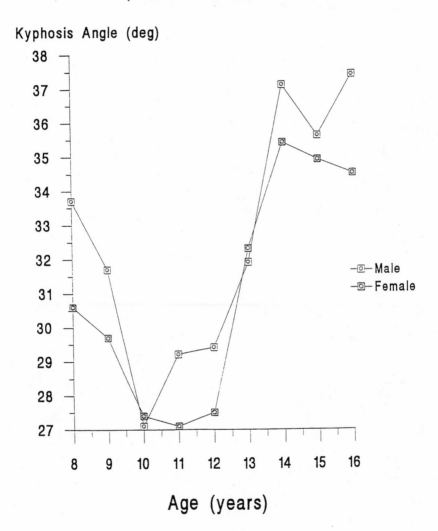

Figure 5.2. Lumbar lordosis during the
growth period in children (Willner & Johnson 1983)

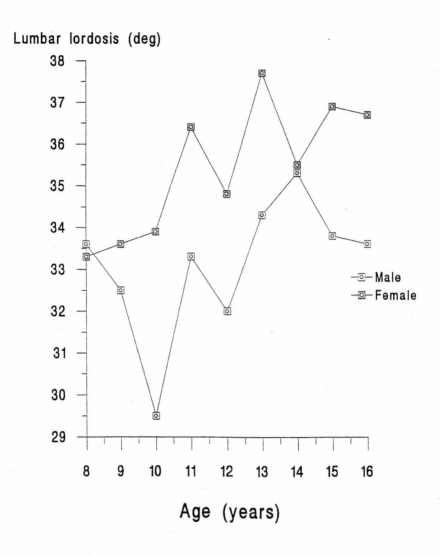

CHAPTER 6 : SIT AND REACH TEST

Purpose of Test :   To measure the flexibility of the hamstrings and lower back.

Common Usages :   Used for both male and female subjects. Ranging in age from 6 year old to maturity and onwards.

Equipment: Sit and reach board box and a yardstick.

Procedures: The subject sits on the floor with legs straight. The subjects arms are extended forward with the hands placed on top of each other to perform the test. The subject reaches directly forward, palms down (elbows extended, wrists pronated and metacarpophalangeal and inter phalangeal joint extended) along the measuring scale on the top panel of the standard test apparatus. It is advisable for the test to be repeated.

Special Notes: Easy to administer in the field and

inexpensive. Trained practitioners are not needed to administer the test. Limitations is that the normal age level differences must be considered. A weakness of the Sit and Reach Test is that the performance may be influenced by the length or width of the body segments. For example an individual having short legs relative to the trunk would have a definite advantage in the sit and reach test. Recent studies have also concluded that it is not a valid test for lower back flexibility in teenage girls. This has also been studied in the male and female population and it was suggested that it is not a good measurement of low back flexibility.

Validity: Acceptable face validity

Reliability: Test-retest reliability ranges from 0.70 to 0.98.

Scoring: The score is the distance in cm from the 'zero' point. The 'zero' point is at 20 cm from the start of the scale so that reaching the toes would gain a score of 20 cm. Positive values occur when the hand is taken past the zero limit. The score taken is the best of 2-4 repetitions.

References:

AAHPERD. *Health-Related Physical Fitness Test Technical Manual*, Washington DC, 1984.

Cheng E.D., Buschbacher P.L., Edlich F.R., Limited joint mobility in power lifters. *The American Journal of Sports Medicine* 16 (3) 280-285, 1988.

Jackson W.A., Baker A.A., The relationship of the sit and reach test to criterion measures of hamstring and back flexibility in young females. *Research Quarterly for Exercise and Sport* 57 (2) 183-186, 1986.

Shepard J.R., Measurement of Fitness The Canadian Experience. *The Journal of Sports Medicine and Physical Fitness* 31 (3) 470-481, 1991.

Simpson S. The Effects of Participation in Physical Education activities upon Health related physical fitness. *The Journal of Human Movement Studies* (17) 153-163, 1989.

Smith JF., Miller C.V. The effect of head position on sit and reach performance. *Research Quarterly for Exercise and Sport* 56 (1), 1985.

Figure 6.1. Gender specific means for sit and reach test

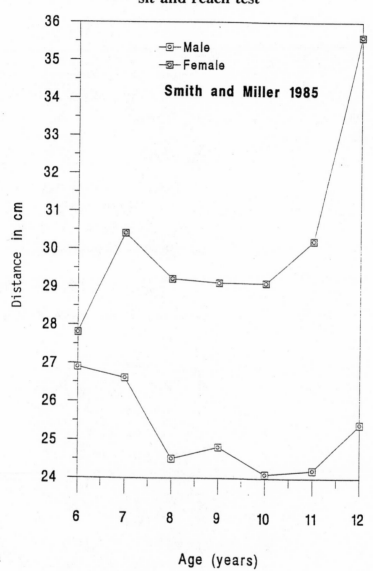

Figure 6.2. Female sit and reach data

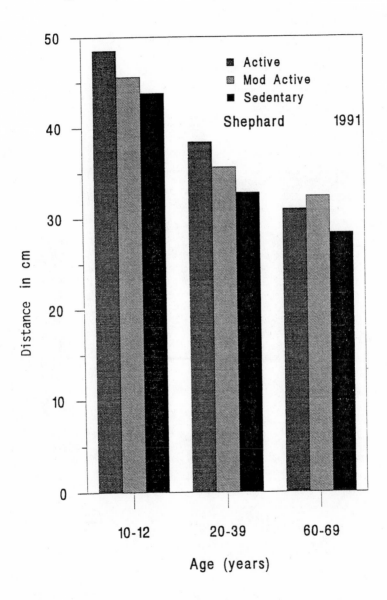

Figure 6.3. Male sit and reach data

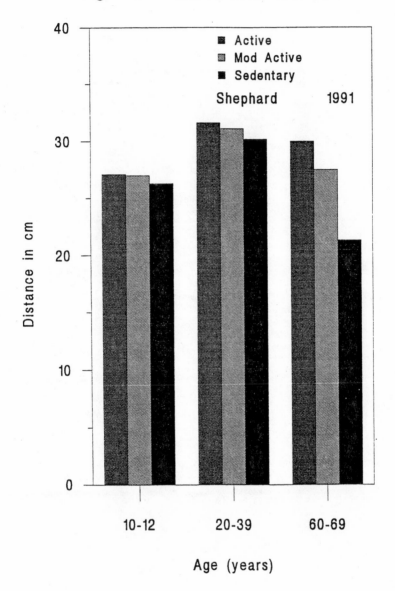

CHAPTER 7 : ISOMETRIC GRIP STRENGTH

Purpose of Test :   Handgrip strength correlates moderately highly with the total strength of 22 other muscles of the body (r = 0.69) (deVries,1980). It therefore gives a reasonable prediction of that individual's total muscular strength. Definition of strength - *"Magnitude of the torque exerted by a muscle or group of muscles in a single, maximal, isometric contraction of restricted duration."* (Enoka, 1988)

Common Usages: Grip strength is important in the elderly because it helps stabilizing when walking down stairs with bannisters.

In the sports environment the test can be used to detect injuries or monitor muscular development in implement sports. It can also be used to calculate total strength by adding the right grip, left grip, leg strength and back strength scores and dividing by body mass. (Heyward, 1991).

Equipment: Hand grip dynamometer with adjustable handle capable of measuring forces between 0 to 100 kilograms, e.g. Stoelting hand grip dynamometer (Stoelting, 1970). Score sheets.

Procedure:

i) Subject stands with arms at the sides.

ii) Grip size is adjusted so that the ring finger's second phalanx is approximately at a right angle.

iii) The dynamometer is held parallel to the side, with the dial facing away from the body.

iv) The subject squeezes the dynamometer with maximum torque.

v) Three trials are administered on each hand alternately with a one minute rest between trials. (Heyward, 1991. Adams, 1990) Equipment should be calibrated regularly.

Validity and Reliability:

Validity is high if criterion activity involves the same isometric contraction. Reliability is 0.9 or better. Subjects may vary in strength, daily between 2 to 12%. Time of day, sleep, drugs, and motivation should be taken into consideration.

Special notes:

i) Subjects should avoid making erratic movements with the dynamometer whilst squeezing.

ii) The technician should record the score and reset the indicator hand of the dynamometer to zero after every trial.

iii) Many variations of dynamometer exist and many have grip adjustments. However, grip size does not effect the score, except in subjects with excessively small or large hands.

iv) Dynamometer comes from the Greek, meaning *"power measure"*. This word is in fact an incorrect description as power is *"the product of force and velocity"* (Enoka, 1988). When recording grip strength there is no velocity element involved, also the moment arm is not taken into account when using power. Therefore a more apt description would be a *"torque measuring device"*.

v) Because strength is directly related to body mass and lean body mass of the individual, the test results should be expressed in relative terms.

vi) The Stoelting dynamometer measures strength as force in kilograms (kg). However, a correct measure of the strength would be torque in newton meters (Nm).

vii) Torque is defined as *"The rotary effect of a force quantified as the product of force and moment arm"*. (Enoka,1988)

Scoring: The mean is taken of the three trials for actual grip strength. The two scores (left and right) are then summed and divided by the individual's body mass. Normal values are presented in figures 7.1 to 7.3. The curves shown in figures 7.1 and 7.2 were based on data fitted with a second order polynomial.

References: Adams G.M. *Exercise physiology laboratory manual.* California State University, Fullerton. Wm

34

C Brown, 1990.

deVries H.A. *Physiology of exercise in physical education and athletics.* Dubuque, Iowa, Wm C Brown, 1980.

Enoka R.M. *Neuromechanical basis of kinesiology.* University of Arizona, Human Kinetics Books, Champaign, Illinois, 1988.

Heyward V.H. *Advanced fitness assessment and exercise prescription,* 2nd Ed. University of New Mexico. Human Kinetics Books, Champaign, Illinois, 1991.

Montoye H.J., Lamphiear D.E. Grip and arm strength in males and females, age 10 to 69. *Research Quarterly.* 48, (1), pp 109-120, 1977.

Stoelting C.H. *Smedley Instruction Manual.* Chicago, 1970.

Figure 7.1: Norms for the sum of right and left grip strengths divided by body mass in males aged 18 to 60 (Montoye and Lamphiear, 1977)

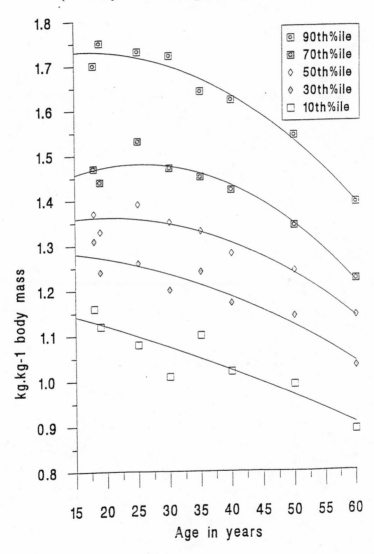

Figure 7.2: Norms for the ratio of the sum of right and left grip strengths to body mass in females aged 18 to 60 (Montoye and Lamphiear, 1977)

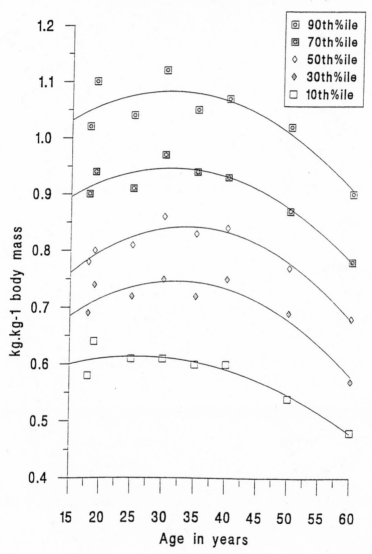

Figure 7.3: Grip strength norms for the strongest
hand in males and females aged 6 to 18 (Adams, 1990)

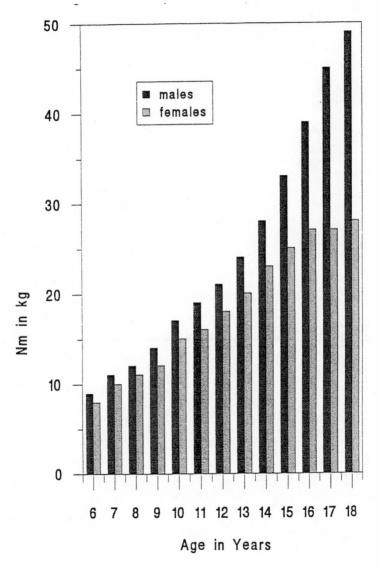

CHAPTER 8 : ISOMETRIC DYNAMOMETRY

Purpose of test: To measure a muscle's maximum potential to produce static force against a resistance, permitting no observable joint movement.

Common Usages: Can be used over a variety of age ranges to measure maximum torque.

Equipment: To perform isometric assessment using an isokinetic dynamometer, a passive dynamometer is required. Passive dynamometers use electromechanical (eg Cybex) or hydraulic (e.g. Akron) components. These dynamometers are capable of isokinetic (concentric), isotonic, or isometric modes of exercise.

Procedure: To measure maximum torque of the quadriceps/ hamstring muscle groups:

The subject should be seated on the dynamometer and be stabilized using straps at both the waist and chest. The stabilizing strap should be fastened across the thigh of the dominant leg, and the arms should be placed across the chest (consistency of position from test to test is important for reliability).

The axis of rotation (in this case the femoral condyle) of the joint being assessed should be aligned as closely as possible with the axis of rotation of the dynamometer. The length of the lever arm should be adjusted so that the shin pad contacts the tibia just above the malleoli of the ankle.

The joint angle should be set to the required position and the subject should be asked to press against the lever arm as hard as possible. The activation need only last for 3-4 seconds. A break (2-3 minutes) should be given before asking the subject to repeat the activation. Whilst testing for maximum isometric torque it is recommended that several different joint angles are tested.

Special notes: One advantage of isometric resistance is that it can be used to assess strength, or to exercise a muscle group around a joint limited in motion by either pathology or bracing. However, isometric strength assessment and exercise are somewhat limited, because they are isolated to a specific point of application within a joint's range of motion (Perrin 1993). One of the strongest angles for the measurement of isometric leg extension or flexion is 50 deg (0 deg = full extension).

Because isometric training sessions are usually of brief duration, there is less depletion of energy stores, and usually less soreness than with isokinetic exercise.

Warning

Isometric activations can produce extreme rises in blood pressure if held more than two to three seconds, and should be avoided by those afflicted with cardiovascular disease.

Validity and reliability:

Face validity accepted, reliability ranges from 0.73 - 0.84.

Scoring:

The maximum amount of torque exerted is recorded and either the best performance, or the average of the best two trials can be used as the measure of static strength.

References:

Lindahl O., Movin A., Rindquist I., Knee extension measurement of the isometric force in different positions of the knee joint. *Acta Orthop. Scandinavia.* 40, 79-85 1969.

Scudder G. N., Torque curves produced at the knee during isometric and isokinetic exercises. *Arch. Phys. Med. Rehabil.* 61, 68-73 1980.

Perrin D.H.   Reliability of isokinetic measures. *Athletic Training*, 10, 319-321, 1986.

Perrin D.H.   Isokinetic exercise and assessment. *Human Kinetics*, Champaign, Illinois 1993.

Figure 8.1: Peak torque for knee extension
using isometric dynamometry

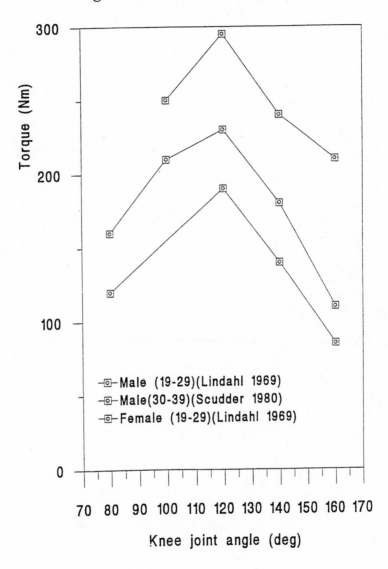

CHAPTER 9 : ISOKINETIC ASSESSMENT

Purpose of test: To measure a muscle's maximum potential to produce force under dynamic conditions, through all or part of a joint's range of motion. The torque can be assessed via both concentric and eccentric modes of activation.

Common Usages: Can be used over a variety of age ranges to measure maximum torque.

Equipment: To perform isokinetic assessment using an isokinetic dynamometer, a passive dynamometer is required for concentric activations and an electromechanical dynamometer with active mechanisms is required to perform eccentric activations. Passive dynamometers use electromechanical (eg Cybex) or hydraulic (e.g. Akron) components. These dynamometers are capable of isokinetic (concentric), isotonic, or isometric modes of exercise.

Test protocol: To measure maximum torque of the

quadriceps/hamstring muscle group:

The subject should be seated on the dynamometer and should be stabilized using straps at both the waist and chest. The arms should be placed across the chest, (consistency of position from test to test is important for reliability).

The axis of rotation of the joint being assessed should be aligned as closely as possible with the axis of rotation of the test or exercise dynamometer. The length of the lever arm should be adjusted so that the shin pad contacts the tibia just above the malleoli of the ankle.

Each test should begin with a warm up session that includes both submaximal and maximal repetitions. Three submaximal (approximately 50% maximal voluntary contraction) and three maximal repetitions have previously been recommended (Johnson and Siegel, 1978), which should be performed before each test velocity.

Concentric testing: Popular concentric isokinetic speeds are 60, 180 and 300 deg.sec^{-1} (slow, medium and fast speed).

The tester should set the machine to 60 deg.sec^{-1} for the first three repetitions, 180 deg. sec^{-1} for the next three repetitions and 300 deg.sec^{-1} for the last three repetitions with approximately 20-30 seconds rest intervals between speed trials. The subject should be instructed to push the lever arm as forcefully and as fast as possible.

The subject should statically stretch the muscle group involved after each session.

Eccentric testing: Popular eccentric isokinetic speeds are 30, 90, 120 and 150 deg.sec^{-1}, although this is sometimes not possible due to the limitations of the dynamometer. The tester should set the machine to 30 deg.sec^{-1} for the first three repetitions. Most dynamometers do not allow testing to commence above 45 deg.sec^{-1} in both passive or eccentric modes. If this is the case, then for each speed above 45 deg.sec^{-1}, the speed should be built up gradually for each testing velocity and the peak torque values only recorded when the required speed is reached.

Three to five repetitions should be performed at each speed. Subjects should be warned that the dynamometer will attempt to push/pull their limb and that they should resist the movement of the lever arm and push forcefully in the opposite direction to the dynamometer. This may take some practice and several attempts should be allowed. If the facility is available, it is recommended that the eccentric activations should be performed in the passive mode

48

Gravity correction: When isokinetic assessment involves movement of a limb though a gravity-dependent position, gravity correction procedures should be employed to account for the weight of the dynamometer's lever arm and the limb being tested.

Validity and reliability: Face validity accepted. Reliability ranges from 0.84 to 0.93 (Perrin 1986).

Scoring: The highest recorded torque produced from each set of three repetitions should be recorded.

Special notes: One advantage of isokinetic resistance is that the muscle group may be exercised to its maximum potential throughout a joint's entire range of motion. Isokinetic exercise is thought to be safer than isotonic or isometric modes because the dynamometer's resistance mechanism essentially disengages when pain or discomfort is experienced by the patient.

Slow velocities should be tested first, this will facilitate motor learning prior to testing at faster velocities (Griffin 1987). One or two days of familiarization and training before actual testing enhances reliability of isokinetic measurement (Kues et al 1992).

For younger subjects it is possible to use the short dynamometer arm usually used for testing the upper extremity of adults.

References:

Alexander M.J.L. Peak torque values for antagonist muscle groups and concentric and eccentric contraction types for elite sprinter. *Archives of Physical Medicine and Rehabilitation.* 71, 334-339, 1990.

Appen L., Duncan P.W. Strength relationship of the knee musculature: Effects of gravity and sport. *Journal of Orthopaedic and Sports Physical Therapy* 6, 293-295, 1985.

Fillyaw M., Bevins T., Fernandez L. Importance of correcting isokinetic peak torque for the effect of gravity when calculating knee flexor or extensor muscle ratios. *Physical Therapy.* 66, 23-29 1986.

Gilliam T.B., Villanacci J.F., Freedson P.S., Sady S.P. Isokinetic torque in boys and girls ages 7 to 13: Effect of age, height and weight. *Research Quarterly.* 50, 599-609, 1979.

Griffin J.W. Differences in elbow flexion torque measured concentrically, eccentrically and isometrically. *Physical Therapy.* 67, 1205-1209, 1987.

Hageman P.A., Gillaspie D.M., Hill L.D. Effects of

speed and limb dominance on eccentric and concentric isokinetic testing of the knee. *Journal of Orthopaedic and Sports Physical Therapy.* *10,* 59-65, 1988.

Hanten W.P., Ramber C.L. Effect of stabilization on maximal isokinetic torque of the quadriceps femoris muscle during concentric and eccentric contractions. *Physical Therapy.* 68, 219-222, 1988.

Henderson R.C., Howes C.L., Erickson K.L., Heere L.M., DeMasi R.A. Knee flexor-extensor strength in children. *Journal of Sports and Physical Therapy.* 18, (4) 599-563, 1993.

Johnson J., Siegel D. Reliability of an isokinetic movement of the knee extensors. *Research Quarterly.* 49, 88-90, 1978.

Knapik J.J., Bauman C.L., Jones B.H., Harris J.M., Vaughan L. Pre-season strength and flexibility imbalances associate with athletic injuries in female collegiate athletes. *American Journal of Sports Medicine.* 19, 76-81, 1991.

Kues J.M., Rothstein Lamb R.L. Obtaining reliable measurements of knee extensor torque produced during maximal voluntary contraction An experimental investigation. *Physical Therapy,* 72,

492-501.

Morris A., Lussier L., Bell G., Dooley J. Hamstring/quadriceps strength ratios in collegiate middle-distance and distance runners. *The Physician and Sportsmedicine.* 11,(10), 71-77, 1983.

Perrin D.H. Reliability of isokinetic measures. *Athletic Training* 10, 319-321, 1986.

Poulmedis P. Isokinetic maximal torque power of Greek elite soccer players. *Journal of Orthopaedic and Sports Physical Therapy.* 6, 293-295, 1985.

Schlinkman B. Norms for high school football players derived from Cybex data reduction computer. *Journal of Orthopaedic and Sports Physical Therapy.* 5, 243-245, 1984.

Westing S.H., Seger J.Y., Karlson E., Ekblom B. Eccentric and concentric torque-velocity characteristics of the quadriceps femoris in man. *European Journal of Applied Physiology.* 58, 100-104, 1988.

Figure 9.1: Peak torque for knee extension
using concentric dynamometry (gravity corrected)

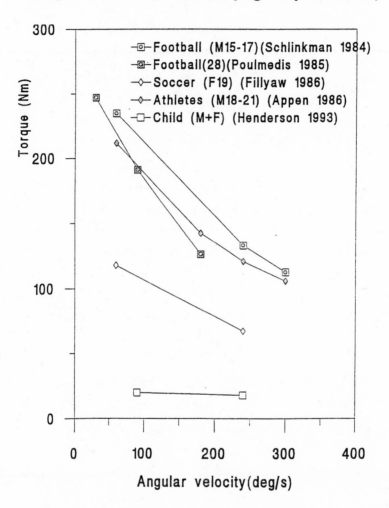

Figure 9.2: Peak torque for knee flexion
using isokinetic dynamometry (gravity corrected)

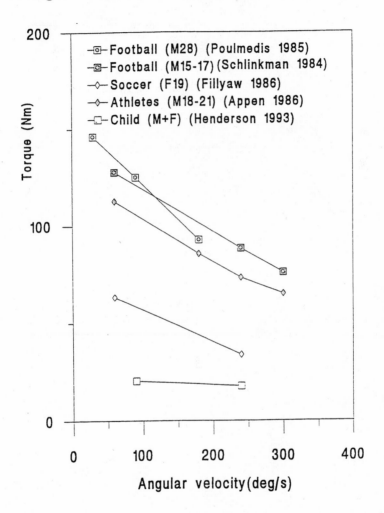

Figure 9.3: Peak torque for knee extension
using isokinetic dynamometry (non-gravity corrected)

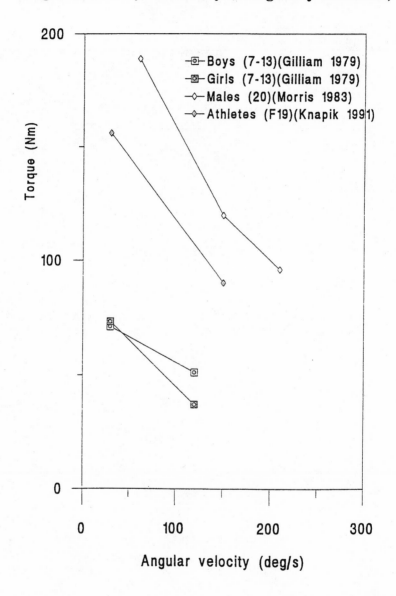

Figure 9.4: Peak torque for knee flexion using concentric isokinetic dynamometry (non-gravity corrected)

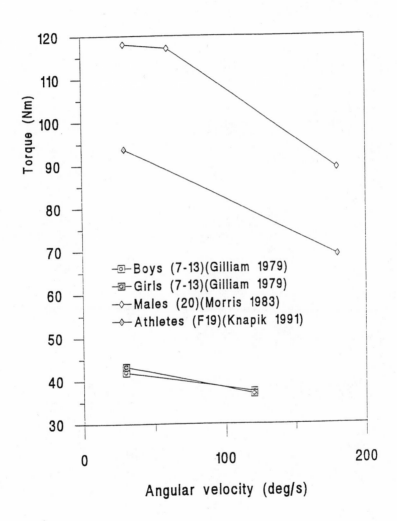

Figure 9.5: Peak torque for knee extension using
eccentric isokinetic dynamometry (non-gravity corrected)

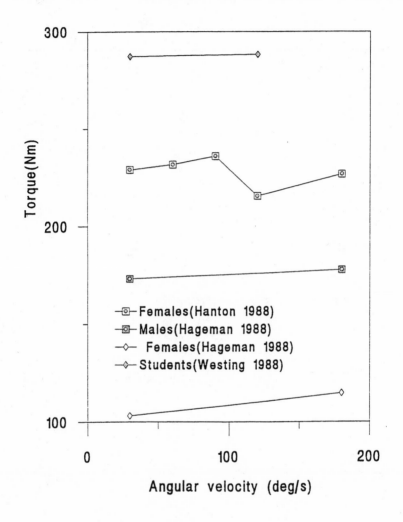

Figure 9.6: Peak torque for knee flexion using eccentric dynamometry (non-gravity corrected)

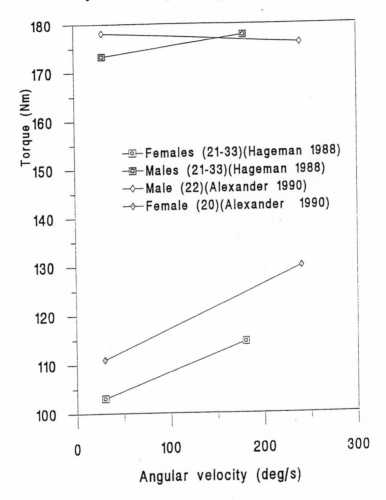

CHAPTER 10 : THE MARGARIA - KALAMEN TEST

Purpose of test: To measure maximal anaerobic leg power.

Common Usages: The Margaria-Kalamen test can be performed from age 10 to old age. However, the maximum age of participation may vary depending on the subject's relative fitness.

Equipment: A staircase with preferably at least 12 steps. The vertical height of each step should be known and be between 0.15 and 0.20 metres. There needs to be a 6 metre run up to the staircase. A stop clock or electric timer with connected switch mats. The timer must be sensitive to 0.01 seconds. An accurate weighing scale.

Procedure: The subject should stand 6 metres in front of the staircase. When ready the subject runs up the stairs as fast as possible, taking 3 stairs at a time. On the 3rd and 9th steps a switch mat is placed. As the subject steps on the 3rd step the clock starts and it stops as (s)he steps on the 9th step. The subject should continue to run flat out until at least the 12th step. The time is recorded to one hundredth of a second. The test should be administered at least 3 times and the best score recorded.

Special notes: The results obtained by this test will vary depending on age, sex and athletic ability.

The degree of motor skill development acquired by a subject appears to play a role in the results of the Margaria-Kalamen test, see table 10.1, (Beckenholdt and Mayhew,1983).

Athletes obtain higher anaerobic power scores than non athletes and untrained adolescent boys have a lower anaerobic power than trained boys, (Armstrong and Ellard,1983).

Research on untrained subjects have showed anaerobic power to be a single factor which is easily measured, but to be associated with both speed and mass. The Margaria-Kalamen test includes body mass in the calculation. Therefore the ability of the individual to manipulate mass becomes critical on the achievement of maximum anaerobic power. The effects of body mass can be minimized by expressing anaerobic power relative to mass, eg.$kgm.s^{-1}$ or $W.kg^{-1}$.

Because anaerobic power scores from the Margaria-

Kalamen test are influenced by body mass it results in a heavier person having a higher score if several individuals achieve the same speed. These findings suggest that heavier persons have a higher developed immediate energy system. There is no direct evidence for this. It is recommended that the Margaria-Kalamen test is used to compare individuals of the same body mass or the same individual over a period of time, e.g. before and after a training programme.

Variations on the Margaria-Kalamen test include the Margaria test using a two-step interval, (Margaria,1966). DeVries (1971) recommended a two-step test using 16 stairs, a 1.8 metre (6ft) run up and the measurements taken between the 2nd and the 6th steps. A variation for younger children was proposed by Chaloupka, described in Johnson and Nelson, (1979). Although the equipment required for this test is minimal, the timing system is relatively expensive. A stop watch can be used instead but then an accurate comparison with the norms cannot be made. If the equipment is available the Margaria-Kalamen test using electronic timing is superior.

Validity and reliability: Face validity is accepted. A correlation of r=0.97 was found between running the 50 yard dash with a 15 yard start and the Margaria-Kalamen test,

(Margaria, 1966). Manning *et al* (1988), found a correlation of r=0.74 between the vertical jump and the Margaria-Kalamen test.

Construct validity is accepted as it has been reported that sprinters have higher scores than middle distance runners and athletes have higher score than non athletes, (Margaria, 1966).

An interclass reliability has been reported to have a correlation of r=0.97, (Baumgartner, 1969).

Stability reliability is likely to be high due to the procedure being repeated at least three times.

Scoring:

Power output can be calculated using the formula:

$$Power = \frac{Work}{Time}$$

Work = Mass x Distance

therefore:

$$Power = \frac{Body\ mass\ x\ distance}{Time}$$

Distance: vertical height between the first and last test steps.

Time: time from the first to last test steps.

Example: 75 kg subject

Distance: 1.05m

Time: 0.49s

Power $=$ $\dfrac{75 \times 1.05}{0.49}$

$= 161$ kgm.s^{-1}.

Some results are expressed in Watts.

1 Watt $= 0.102$ kgm.s^{-1}.

References:

Armstrong N., and Ellard R. The measurement of alactacid anaerobic power in trained and untrained adolescent boys. *Physical Education Review,* 6(2) 150-156, 1983.

Baumgartner T.A. Estimating reliability when all test trials are administered on the same day. *Research Quarterly,* 40, 222-225, 1969.

Beckenholdt S.E., and Mayhew J.L. Specificity among anaerobic power tests in male athletes. *Journal of Sports Medicine,* 23, 326-323, 1983.

DeVries H.A. *Laboratory experiments in physiology of exercise.* Wm Brown, Dublique. Iowa, 101-104, 1971.

Fox E.L., and Mathews,D.K. *The physiological basis of physical education and athletics* (3rd Edition) W.B.Saunders, Philadelphia, 619-625, 1981.

Johnson B.L., and Nelson J.K. *Practical measurements for evaluation in physical education* (3rd Edition) Burgess Co. Minneapolis, 4-61, 1079.

Kalamen J. *Measurement of maximum power in man.* Ohio State University, Ohio, 1968.

Kirkendall D.R., Gruber J.J., and Johnson R.E. *Measurement and evaluation for physical educators* (2nd Edition) Human Kinetics Publishers, Inc. Champaign, Illinois, 1987.

McArdle W.D., Katch F.I., and Katch B.L. *Exercise physiology, energy, nutrition and human performance* (3rd Edition) Lea and Febiger, Philadelphia/London, 1991.

Manning J.M., and Dooly Manning C. Factor analysis of various anaerobic power tests. *Journal of Sports Medicine* 28 138-144, 1988.

Margaria R *et al.* Measurement of muscular power (anaerobic) in man. *Journal of Applied Physiology*, 21: 1662-1664, 1966.

Table 10.1: Power measurements of male athletes

SPORT	POWER (W.kg^{-1})
Football	20.0
Wrestling	19.8
Basketball	19.3
Baseball	19.1
Soccer	18.4

(Adapted from Beckenholdt and Mayhew, 1983)

Table 10.2: Normal values for males on the Margaria-Kalamen test in kgm.s^{-1}.

CLASSIF-ICATION	15-20 years	20-30 years	30-40 years	40-50 years	Over 50
Poor	Under 113	Under 106	Under 85	Under 65	Under 50
Fair	113-149	106-139	85-111	65-84	50-65
Average	150-187	140-175	112-140	85-104	66-82
Good	188-224	176-210	141-168	106-125	83-98
Excellent	Over 224	Over 210	Over 125	Over 125	Over 98

(Source: Kalamen,1968 and Margaria, 1966)

CHAPTER 11 : THE VERTICAL JUMP TEST

Purpose of test: To measure maximal anaerobic leg power.

Common usages: The vertical jump test is suitable from nine years of age for both males and females.

Equipment: Although electronic equipment can be used, the following is adequate.

A wall or post to support a flat measuring board of about 30cm long and 15cm wide. Chalk or chalk dust to mark the peak jump. Accurate weighing scales. A stadiometer or anthropometer to measure the subject's height.

Procedure: The subject's mass should be recorded. Prior to the test commencing it is advisable to exercise for about 5-10 minutes. This should include warming up, stretching and finishing with a few half to three quarter effort vertical jumps.

The subject should position him/herself with the

dominant side towards the wall and feet together. The opposite arm should be placed behind the back. The dominant hand should be chalked and with the arm towards the wall the subject reaches as far as possible by standing on his/her toes. The highest point marked by the middle finger should be recorded.

The subject should adapt his/her feet ready to jump as no further feet or arm movement is allowed during the jump, other than the one dip of the knees. A full squat position is adopted and once balanced a maximum jump is made. The wall is touched with the arm fully extended at the height of the jump. The highest point is recorded. Three trials are given with the best score being recorded. The best score is the greatest distance between the two chalk marks.

Special notes:

For the vertical jump test to be a true estimate of leg power, the subject's body mass should be included in the calculation. The Lewis nomogram is designed to include body mass and thus gives more accurate measurement.

The norms included in Table 11.1 are for the test as described here. Lower scores can be found on tests with more restrictive jumping procedures. This includes Gray et al's (1962), method, where the dominant reach arm must remain in the elevated position during the preparatory and jump phases. Athletes have been found to have higher values than non athletes and males to have higher values than females, (Costill and Miller, 1968; Baumgartner and Jackson, 1987; AAPHER, 1966 and Adams,1990). Table 11.2 shows the results of studies using this method.

There are a limited number of norms expressed in true anaerobic power units i.e. kgm.s^{-1}. Results not expressed relative to body mass are not a true prediction of anaerobic power between subjects of different masses.

Validity and Reliability: Face validity is accepted. A validity coefficient of r=0.78 has been reported for a comparison between the vertical jump test and the sum of four track and field event scores, (Johnson and Nelson, 1974).

A correlation has been reported of r=0.74 between the vertical jump and the Margaria-Kalamen tests and a correlation of r=0.79 between the vertical jump and the standing jump tests, (Baumgartner, 1969).

Studies on the test-retest reliability of the vertical jump have shown a correlation of r=0.93 for this technique, (Johnson and Nelson, 1974). A correlation of r=0.99 was found when testing University students, (Considine and Sullivan, 1972).

Latchew (1954), found a correlation of r=0.90-0.97 when testing children. This suggests that the stability reliability is very high.

Scoring:

The distance between the two chalk markers should be recorded. To convert this score into a power value (kgm.s^{-1}) the following equation can be used:

Power = 2.21 x Wt/D

where 2.21 = a constant based on the law of falling bodies.

Wt = body mass in kg of the subject in jumping clothes.

D= the distance between the 2 chalk marks in metres.

e.g. a 75kg subject

D= 44.6 cm

Power = 2.21 x 75 / 0.466

=110.7 kgm.s^{-1}

It can be converted to Watts using:

1W = 0.102 kgm.s^{-1}.

e.g. 110.7 kgm.s^{-1} = 1085.3 W

$$= \frac{1085.3}{75}$$

= 14.7 W.kg^{-1}

An alternative method is to use the Lewis nomogram (Mathews and Fox 1976 p500). This is used by placing a straight edge from the distance line to the mass line. Where the straight line crosses the anaerobic power line the score is given in kgm.s^{-1}.

References:

AAPHER, *Skills test manual: Basketball for boys.* Washington D.C. AAHPHER, 1966.

AAPHER, *Skills test manual: Basketball for girls.* Washington D.C. AAHPHER, 1966.

Adams G.M. *Exercise physiology laboratory manual.* Wm C Brown, California State University. Fullerton, 1990.

Adams G.M. Vertical jumps of college physical education majors. Unpublished raw data, 1981.

Baumgartner T.A. Estimating reliability when all the test trials are administered on the same day. *Research Quarterly,* 40, 222-225, 1969.

Baumgartner T.A. and Johnson A.B. *Measurement for evaluation in physical education and exercise science.* Wm C Brown, Dubuque, Iowa, 1987.

Beckenholdt S.E. and Mayhew J.L. Specifity among anaerobic power tests in male athletes. *Journal of Sports Medicine ,*23, 326-332, 1983.

Considine W.J. and Sullivan W.J. Relationship of selected tests of leg strength and leg power on college men. *Research Quarterly* 44, (4), 404-416, 1973.

Costill D.L. and Miller S.J. Relationship among selected tests of explosive leg strength and power. *Research Quarterly*, 39, (3) 785, 1968.

Friermood H.T. *Volleyball skills contest for Olympic development in United States volleyball association, annual official volleyball rules and reference guide of the U.S. volleyball association,* Berne, Ind: USUBA. 134-135, 1967.

Gray R.K., Start K.B. and Glencross D.J. A test of leg power. *Research Quarterly,* 33, (1) 44, 1962.

Johnson B.L., and Nelson J.K. *Practical measurements for evaluation in physical education.* Burgess, Minnaepolis, Minnesota, 1974.

Kirkendall D.R., Gruber J.J., and Johnson R.E. *Measurement and evaluation for physical educators* (3rd Edition), Human Kinetics, Champaign, Illinois, 1982.

Latchew M. Measuring selected motor skills in fourth, fifth and sixth grades. *Research Quarterly,*

25, (4) 404-416, 1963.

Manning J.M., et al. Factor analysis of various anaerobic power tests. *Journal of Sports Medicine,* 28, 138-144, 1988.

Mathews D.K., and Fox E.L. *The physiological basis of physical education and athletics.* W.B. Saunders, Philadelphia, 1976.

McArdle W.D., Katch F.I., and Katch V.L. *Exercise physiology, energy, nutrition and human performance* (3rd Edition), Lea and Febiger, Philadelphia/London, 1991.

Table 11.1: Vertical jump in cm for height percentile values for males (M) and females (F) of different ages.

HEIGHT PERCENTILES

SEX	AGE	90	70	50	30	10	0
M AND F	9-11.	15	12	10	7	2	0
M	12-14.	18	16	13	9	2	0
F	12-14.	15	13	11	8	2	0
M	15-17.	23	21	16	8	2	0
F	15-17.	16	14	11	6	2	0
M	18-34.	25	23	16	9	2	0
F	18-34.	13	12	8	4	1	0

(Source: Friermood, 1967).

Table 11. 2: Height differences in centimetres of different athletic groups.

SAMPLE	AGE	50TH PERCENTILE	SOURCE
College Footballer	Adult	20.9	Baumgartner and Johnson,1987
Average Male	Adult	19.5	Baumgartner and Johnson,1987
Female PE major	Adult	15.0	Baumgartner and Johnson,1987
Average Female	Adult	13.0	Baumgartner and Johnson,1987
Male	17	19.5	Baumgartner and Johnson,1987
Female	17	13.0	Baumgartner and Johnson,1987
Male	17-18	20.0	AAPHER,1966
Female	17-18	13.0	AAPHER,1966
Male	18-34	16.0	Johnson and Nelson,1974
Female	18-34	8.0	Johnson and Nelson,1974

Figure 11.1: Mean values for the vertical jump test.
(Source: Friermood, 1967)

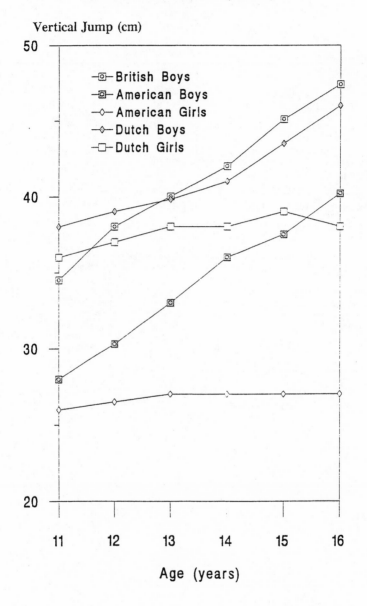

CHAPTER 12 : WINGATE ANAEROBIC POWER TEST

Purpose of test: To measure the anaerobic power and anaerobic capacity of the legs or arms.

Common usages: Most results are presented for males and females between the ages of 18-28.

Equipment: A mechanically braked cycle ergometer (eg Monark) is required. Constant power ergometers are not suitable. A device to count pedal revolutions automatically is needed. A stop watch is required to record time and a set of scales is needed to measure body mass. A microcomputer interfaced with the revolution counter (eg a BBC microcomputer model B+). Relevant software is required to calculate power output. The CONCEPT II software package is effective. This is available from *CONCEPT II , 151-153 Nottingham Road, Old Basford, Nottingham N66 0FU.*

Procedure: The basic test protocol requires 10-12 minutes to perform correctly. Warm up cycling is required, usually for 5 minutes. This involves cycling at a low intensity interspersed with 4-5 sprints of 4-6 seconds duration. A recovery period of 2-5 minutes should then precede the test. The test starts with a 15 second acceleration period at 33% of the prescribed load, building up to 100% of the prescribed load. The test begins when the prescribed load reaches 100%. An all out sprint for 30 seconds then follows. After the test has been completed a cool down period of 1-2 minutes is required, usually by cycling at a low to moderate aerobic level. The prescribed load can be calculated using the equation **0.075 x body mass = load (kg).** Computations through the software give values for anaerobic power (average power), relative anaerobic capacity, total work (kJ), peak power (W) and the time to peak power (sec), minimum power (W) and the time to minimum power and the fatigue index $(W.sec^{-1})$.

Special notes: The test can also be performed for the upper body using an identical procedure. The only difference is that an arm crank ergometer is required. The equation to predict load is also modified. Body mass is now multiplied by 0.05. Due to the nature of the equipment, malfunctions do occur. These should be minimised by regularly checking the equipment. Spare equipment should also be available. The test can be administered to approximately five subjects per hour.

Validity and reliability: When compared to blood lactate levels a moderate relationship was found (r=0.60). This however is not conclusive evidence but physiological validity was found when compared with the area of fast twitch muscle fibres in the leg (r=-0.91). Reliability (test-retest) co-efficients were high, ranging from 0.95 - 0.98.

Scoring: Anaerobic capacity and relative anaerobic capacity can be compared to percentile figures. The fatigue index is a measure of endurance. Generally the smaller the figure the greater the subject endurance.

References: Adams G.M. *Exercise Physiology Laboratory Manual.* Wm.C. Brown, 1990.

Bar-Or O. The Wingate anaerobic test. An update on methodology, reliability and validity. *Sports Medicine* 4, 381-394, 1987.

Figure 12.1: Percentile norms for aerobic capacity
in men and women aged between 18-28.
Data from Adams (1990)

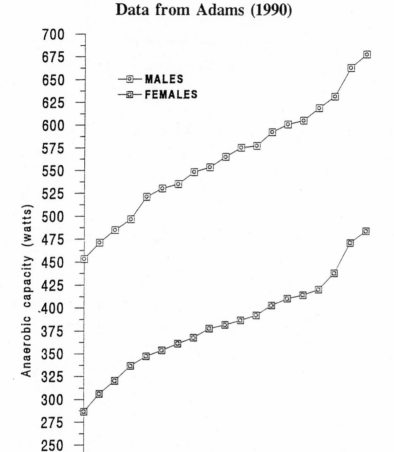

Figure 12.2: Percentile norms for relative anaerobic capacity (watts per kilogram) for males and females aged between 18-28.

Data from Adams (1990)

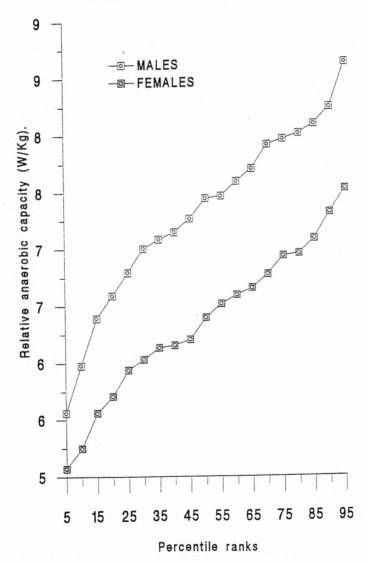

CHAPTER 13 : STANDING BROAD (LONG) JUMP

Purpose of test: To measure anaerobic power of the legs in jumping forward.

Common usages: Results are presented for males and females from the age of six through to college age.

Equipment: A flat surface (e.g. the floor) is required for this test. Marking material, either tape or chalk is required to be used as a starting line. A tape measure is also needed to mark off increments in distance along the landing area.

Procedure: With the feet parallel to each other and behind the starting line the performer bends the knees, swings the arms and jumps forward as far as possible along the landing area. Practice trials may be performed. Three test trials are performed, the best score (longest distance) is recorded.

Special notes: If the performer falls backward upon landing, then the nearest mark to the start line is taken as the measurement. Practice trials should be encouraged until the task can be performed successfully. This will improve validity and reliability.

Validity and reliability: Validity has been measured using a pure power test as the criterion. An "r" value as high as 0.61 was reported. AAHPERD (1976) reported that the test was generally accepted as a measure of explosive power.

Reliability has been reported as high as 0.99 (AAHPERD, 1976).

Scoring: Scores are presented in percentile form. The greatest distance between the heel and the start line is used and rounded to the nearest centimetre. This figure is then referred to the relevant table and a percentile score is given.

Reference: AAHPERD, Youth fitness test manual, Washington DC AAHPERD (1976).

Figure 13.1: Percentile ranks for the female standing broad jump distances for different ages.

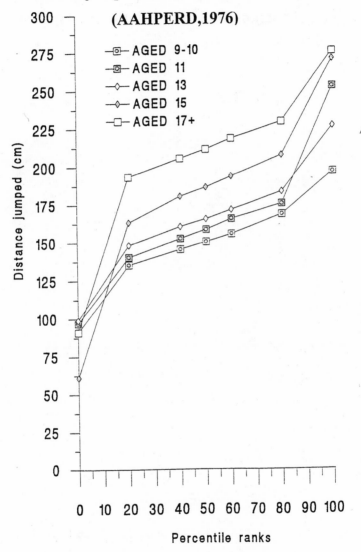

Figure 13.2: Percentile ranks for the male standing broad jump distances for different ages.

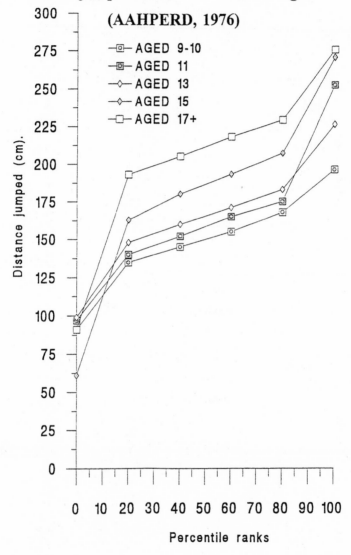

(AAHPERD, 1976)

CHAPTER 14 : PROGRESSIVE TREADMILL TEST

Purpose: To measure aerobic capacity, (sometimes called aerobic power, cardiovascular endurance, circulorespiratory endurance and cardiorespiratory endurance).

Common Usages: Treadmill tests account for about 70% of all maximum tests. The Bruce protocol is the most common of these (Pollock *et al* 1984). Most results are presented for males and females (aged 10 to 60), but the first stages of the protocol have been used in younger children (4 years old) and in clinical settings (Cumming *et al* 1978). It is flexible enough to be used in diverse populations e.g. cardiac patients, sedentary to active and young to middle-aged populations (Pollock *et al* 1984).

The results of maximum oxygen uptake tests (VO_2max) can be used to demonstrate the role of the cardiorespiratory system in the transportation of oxygen, measure changes in aerobic capacity over time and indicate potential in endurance events (Adams 1990).

Equipment: Stadiometer and levelled platform scales. Thermometer and barometer. Heart rate monitor. Stopwatch. Calibrated motorized treadmill. Noseclip. Rubber mouthpiece. Rudolph valve. Ventilatory hoses. Metabolic gas analysis system interfaced with a computer and a printer (e.g. The University of Liverpool Totally Integrated Metabolic Analyzer) (Brodie *et al* 1994). Head-harness or hoist to support mouthpiece. Paper towels. Disinfectant.

The equipment forms an open circuit spirometry system. The equipment is set up following the procedure of Adams (1990 pp.68-72).

Procedure: Before testing the metabolic analyzer must be calibrated, the equipment checked and the ambient air sampled. The ambient concentrations of oxygen and carbon dioxide, temperature and barometric pressure are recorded. At least three testers are needed for the test to be carried out safely and effectively. One should supervise the metabolic analyzer, one the speed and gradient of the treadmill and the other the safety and requirements of the subject. At least one tester should have a knowledge of cardiopulmonary resuscitation.

The subject should be in a normally hydrated condition, not have eaten a meal within the last three hours or be under the influence of drugs. The subject should be dressed in appropriate light weight clothing and running shoes and not have any signs or symptoms of contraindications to maximal exercise testing (American College of Sports Medicine 1986 pp.13-14).

The subject's informed written consent should be obtained. In the case of minors the parent or legal guardian must provide the consent. The Bruce test protocol and purpose are fully explained.

The subject stands on a combined stadiometer and levelled platform scale. With the subject's head in the Frankfort plane (Lohman *et al* 1988) height (cm) and mass (kg) are recorded.

The age predicted maximum heart rate for the subject is calculated using the following equation:

Max Heart Rate (beats·min^{-1}) = 220 - age (years)

The subject is familiarised with the equipment. A heart rate monitor is fitted around the chest. On entering the treadmill the subject stands with legs astride it and holds onto the handrails. If headgear is used to support the mouthpiece and tubing it is adjusted until it fits tightly yet comfortably. If it is supported by a harness then it is checked to ensure stability. The rubber mouthpiece is placed in the subject's mouth and its comfort is assessed and checked to ensure it allows adequate ventilation. A noseclip is placed on the nose. Throughout the test procedure the subject is unable to speak and informs the testers of "comfort" with a thumbs up signal and "discomfort" with a thumbs down signal.

When the subject is adequately prepared the treadmill is started with the subject in the middle, feet astride of the moving belt and holding on to the handrails. One foot is placed on the belt and then moved back to its original position to enable the subject to set a steady rhythm and the most natural walking pace. When the subject feels secure the other foot is placed on the treadmill and begins to walk while still in support. If at any time the subject needs to get off the treadmill, such as at maximal volitional exhaustion, the subject grabs the handrails in support and then straddles the moving belt.

The subject should look straight ahead while on the treadmill and not at the moving belt as this may induce nausea. When 2.7 $k \cdot hr^{-1}$ and 10% gradient are reached the first level of the Bruce protocol begins and the timer is started. The fraction of expired oxygen (F_{EO2}), carbon dioxide (F_{ECO2}) and the volume of expired air ($V_{E)}$) are recorded every

30 seconds.

The Bruce test involves seven stages of three minute periods of exercise on the treadmill. At the end of each three minute period the work load is intensified by increasing the speed and gradient (see Table 14.1). As the test progresses the subject is given verbal encouragement to maintain motivation.

The test continues until maximal volitional exhaustion occurs, heart rate reaches the age predicted maximum or the end of level 7. If the subject stops before the end of the test the time is noted. The nose clip and mouthpiece are removed. A recovery period is given at the same speed and gradient as level 2 and when completed the subject exits the treadmill. The testers should confirm with the subject that adequate recovery has occurred and give a briefing on the results when they are known.

The metabolic calculations are performed by the computer interfaced with the metabolic analyzer. Gas readings are automatically converted from ATPS (Atmospheric Temperature Pressure and Saturate) to the universal volumes of STPD (Standard Pressure Temperature and Dry). This provides measurements for every 30s of the test for the percentage of O_2 and CO_2 in expired air, the absolute volume of O_2 inspired ($V_I O_2$ in $l \cdot min^{-1}$) and CO_2 expired ($V_E CO_2$ in $l \cdot min^{-1}$), the RER

(Respiratory Exchange Ratio), the volume of air expired (V_E in $l \cdot min^{-1}$), heart rate (beats $\cdot min^{-1}$) and the relative volume of oxygen consumption (VO_2 in $ml \cdot min^{-1} \cdot kg^{-1}$).

A graph can be printed with duration of the test plotted against the volume of oxygen consumed. VO_2 max can be inferred from the curve at the point where VO_2 consumption begins to plateau. If it does not plateau then the highest or peak VO_2 can be used. Other indicators that VO_2 max has occurred are an RER greater than 1.0 and blood lactate measurements of between 70-80mg lactate per 100ml (Shephard 1984).

Special Notes: It appears that adult males and females find the pacing of the speeds awkward at levels 4 and 3 respectively. Individuals with extremely large aerobic capacities may have difficulty in reaching VO_2max using the Bruce test.

The test can be modified to include two three minute stages at the beginning. The first at 2.74 $k \cdot hr^{-1}$ with 0% gradient and the second at 2.74 $k \cdot hr^{-1}$ with 5% gradient (Pollock *et al* 1984).

A lower level 12 minute test has been designed for subjects with low fitness (Lerman *et al* 1976). It involves four stages of three minutes. This is important especially for elderly subjects (over 65 years of age). The second level of the Bruce test corresponds to 7 METs which is at or near the VO_2max of most elderly people.

If an integrated metabolic analyzer is not available a two way valve and Douglas bags can be used to collect exhaled air in the last minute of each level of exercise during steady state. This is analyzed for the fractions of expired O_2 and CO_2 using a metabolic analyzer and the volume is determined by a dry gas volumeter. Calculations must be performed manually (Adams 1990 pp.72-76) to determine VO_2max or appropriate software packages can be used.

Validity and reliability: VO_2max represents the largest amount of oxygen that can be utilized under strenuous activity. Over a wide range of dynamic exercise there is a high correlation between cardiac output and VO_2 (McArdle *et al* 1991). VO_2max generally summarizes what is happening in the oxygen transport system in maximal exercise and is credited as a measure of aerobic capacity (Pollock et al 1984). The Bruce protocol has both construct and empirical validity.

Reliability as high as 0.99 (SEE $= \pm$ 1.9 ml·kg^{-1}·min^{-1}) in healthy men and women and 0.95 in stable cardiac patients has been reported (Bruce *et al* 1973). In children high reliability of 0.96 has also been reported (Cumming *et al* 1978).

Scoring: The score is the maximum amount of oxygen that can be consumed within one minute expressed in absolute terms ($l \cdot min^{-1}$) or relative to body weight ($ml \cdot kg^{-1} \cdot min^{-1}$).

Table 14.1 The Bruce treadmill exercise protocol

Stage	Time minutes	Speed mph kph	Gradient %	Average O_2 cons. ml/kg/min	METS*
1	3	1.7 2.74	10	18	4.6
2	6	2.5 4.02	12	25	7.0
3	9	3.4 5.47	14	36	10.2
4	12	4.2 6.76	16	46	12.1
5	15	5.0 8.05	18	56	14.9
6	18	5.5 8.86	20	63	17.0
7	21	6.0 9.66	22	70	19.3
recovery	24	2.5 4.02	12	-	-

Adapted from Adams (1990 p.71), Heyward (1991 p.40) Balogun and Ladipo (1989 p.109), Cumming *et al* (1978 p.70), Bruce *et al* (1973 p.547) and Kasser and Bruce (1969 p.761).

* 1 MET is approximately equal to 3.5 $ml \cdot kg^{-1} \cdot min^{-1}$ of O_2 uptake (American College of Sports Medicine 1986).

Table 14.2 Ranges of maximum oxygen consumption values for males and females involved in different sports.

Sport	Males VO$_2$max (ml^{-1}kg-1min^{-1})	Females VO$_2$max (ml^{-1}kg-1min^{-1})
American football	48-54	-
Athletics field events	46-54	40-50
Athletics track events	60-80	50-70
Baseball/softball	48-54	40-46
Basketball	44-50	40-46
Race bicycling	65-72	48-56
Canoeing	60-68	54-60
Gymnastics	50-58	-
Ice Hockey	52-60	-
Jockey	52-60	46-52
Orienteering	48-58	-
Cross country skiing	66-80	58-70
Ski jumping	66-72	-
Soccer	54-62	-
Speed Skating	58-74	48-56
Swimming	56-70	48-64
Volleyball	50-60	46-56
Weight lifting	40-50	-
Wrestling	54-65	-

Adapted from Wasserman *et al* (1987 p.38)

References:

Adams G.M. *Exercise Physiology Laboratory Manual.* Wm.C. Brown Publishers, Dubuque, Illinois, 1990.

American College of Sports Medicine. *Guidelines for Exercise Testing and Prescription.* Third Edition, Lea and Febiger, Philadelphia, 1986.

Balogun M.O. and Ladipo G.O. Cardiovascular responses to maximal treadmill exercise in healthy adult Nigerians. *African Journal of Medicine and Medical Science,* 18, 109-116, 1989.

Bruce R.A., Kusumi F. and Hosmer D. Maximal oxygen intake and nomographic assessment of functional aerobic impairment in cardiovascular disease. *American Heart Journal,* 85, (4), 546-560, 1973.

Convertino V.A., Sather T.M., Goldwater D.J. and Alford W.R. Aerobic fitness does not contribute to production of othostatic intolerance. *Medicine and Science in Sport and Exercise,* 18, (5), 551-556, 1986.

Cumming G.R., Everatt D. and Hastman L. Bruce treadmill test in children: normal values in a clinical population. *The American Journal of Cardiology,*

41, 69-75, 1978.

Heyward V.H. *Advanced Fitness Assessment and Exercise Prescription*. Second Edition, pp.18-69. Human Kinetics Books, Champaign, Illinois, 1991.

Holloszoy J.O. Exercise, health, and aging: a need for more information. *Medicine and Science in Sports and Exercise*, 15, (1), 1-5, 1983.

Hudson D.L., Smith M.L. and Raven P.B. Physical fitness and haemodynamic response of women to lower body negative pressure. *Medicine and Science in Sport and Exercise*, 19, (4), 375-381, 1987.

Kasser I.S. and Bruce R.A. Comparative effects of aging and coronary heart disease on submaximal and maximal exercise. *Circulation*, 39, 759-774, 1969.

Lerman J., Bruce R.A., Sivarajan E., Pettet G.E.M. and Trimble S. Low-level dynamic exercises for earlier cardiac rehabilitation: aerobic and hemodynamic responses. *Archives of Physical Medicine and Rehabilitation*, 57, 355-360, 1976.

Lohman T.G., Roche A.F. and Reynaldo M. (Eds.). *Anthropometric Standardization Reference*

Manual, Human Kinetics Books, Chaimpaign, Illinois, 1988.

McArdle W.D., Katch F.I. and Katch V.L. *Exercise Physiology: Energy, Nutrition, and Human Performance*. Third Edition, Lea and Febiger, Philadelphia, 1991.

Pollock M.L., Bohamon R.L., Cooper K.H., Ayres J.J., Ward A., White S.R. and Linneurd A.C. A comparative of four protocols for maximal treadmill testing. *American Heart Journal* 92,(1), 39-46, 1976.

Pollock M.L., Foster C., Schmidt D., Hellman C., Linnerud A.C. and Ward A. Comparative analysis of physiological responses to three different maximal graded exercise test protocols in healthy women. *American Heart Journal*. 103, 363-373, 1982.

Pollock M.L., Wilmore J.H. and Fox S.M. *Exercise in Health and Disease: Evaluation and Prescription for Prevention and Rehabilitation*. W.B. Saunders Company, Philadelphia, 1984.

Shephard R.J. Tests of maximal oxygen intake: a critical review. *Sports Medicine*, 1, 99-124, 1984.

Skinner J.S. *Exercise Testing and Exercise Prescription for Special Cases: Theoretical Basis and Clinical Application.* Lea and Febiger, Philadelphia, 1987.

Smith M.L., Hudson A.L., Graitzer H. and Raven P.B. Vasoconstrictor response to lower body negative pressure during autonomic blockade: effect of fitness. (Abstract) *Medicine and Science in Sport and Exercise*, 18(Suppl):S15, 1986.

Wasserman K., *et al.* Determinants and detection of anaerobic threshold and consequences of exercise above it. *Circulation*, 76: 29-39, 1987.

Figure 14.1: Cardiorespiratory fitness classifications of maximal oxygen uptake values for different age groups of American males.

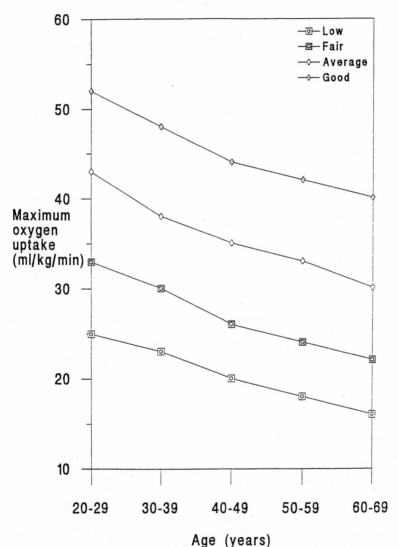

Adapted from the American Heart Association (1972 p.15) and Heyward (1991 p.26).

Figure 14.2: Cardiorespiratory fitness classifications of maximum oxygen uptake values for different age groups of American females.

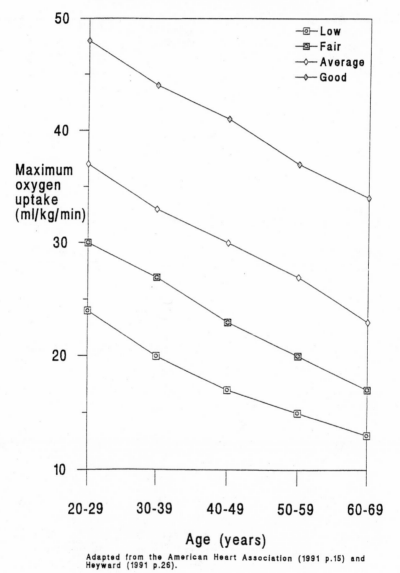

Adapted from the American Heart Association (1991 p.15) and Heyward (1991 p.26).

Figure 14.3: A comparison of mean maximum volume of oxygen consumption values between different age groups of American and Nigerian males and females.

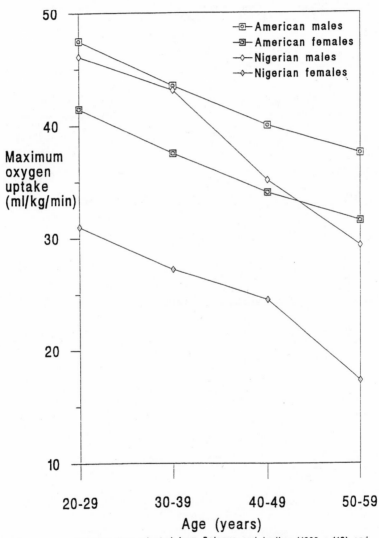

Nigerian data adapted from Balogun and Ladipo (1989 p.112) and American data adapted from Wasserman et al (1987 p.38).

Figure 14.4: The mean oxygen consumption values for different mean ages of men from studies using the Bruce treadmill test.

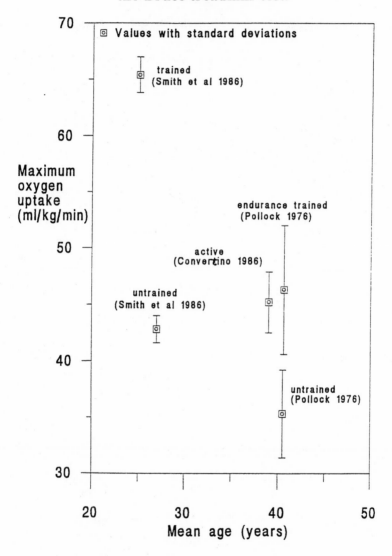

Figure 14.5: The mean maxiumum oxygen consumption values for different mean ages of females from studies using the Bruce treadmill test.

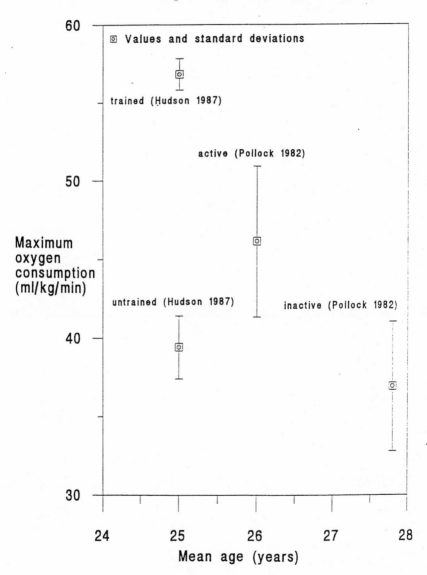

CHAPTER 15 : THE HARVARD STEP TEST.

Purpose of test: To estimate cardiovascular fitness using recovery heart rate values.

Common uses: Normal values recorded for young adults. Initially designed for young males (aged 19-24), Brouha (1943). Modified data available for young female subjects, Bonen (1975).

Equipment: Bench 50cm high (20 inches).
Stopwatch or clock.
Metronome.

Procedure: The subject steps up onto the 50cm bench, firstly with the left foot followed by the right foot. Once standing completely upright on the bench, both legs straight, the subject steps down off the bench onto the floor. Loading throughout the cycle is upon the left leg, it must be remembered that the left leg continually leads, Adams (1990).

The metronome is set to the desired cadence of 30

steps per minute. An exercise duration time of five minutes is required. Subjects unable to complete the test prior to the five minute period may stop at any time, at which point the recovery period starts, Bandyopadhyay and Chattopadhay (1981). As soon as the test is completed the subject must then adopt a sitting position. The pulse is then taken during the recovery period. Pulse readings are taken at 1 to 1.5 minutes, 2 to 2.5 minutes and 3 to 3.5 minutes. For methods of pulse reading see special notes below.

Special notes: When taking pulse readings to determine heart rate, palpate the pulse at the carotid artery, (in the neck just lateral of the larynx) use the tip of the middle and index fingers. Do not use the thumb as it has its own pulse which may cause inaccurate readings, Heyward (1991). Do not apply heavy pressure to the artery as this may reduce the heart rate readings. Count the pulse for thirty seconds, at the time intervals indicated above. An alternative shorter procedure based on the Harvard Step Test can be used. This test is identical in procedure as described above except, (1) the duration is shortened to 3 minutes, (2) the bench height is reduced to 45cm (18 inches), (3) cadence is set to 24 steps. min^{-1}, Toriola and Mathur (1986).

Scoring procedure: The three half minute pulse readings are totalled and used in the following equation. This calculates the physical fitness index (PFI). Pulse readings are also taken if the subject fails to complete the full testing period and the PFI is calculated in the same way.

$$PFI = \frac{\text{duration of exercise (sec) x 100.}}{2 \text{ x sum of recovery heart rates.}}$$

Other information: The advantages of using this test is that it is possible to administer to a large number of subjects in the field situation, without requiring expensive equipment and trained testers. This test uses post exercise recovery rate values for aerobic fitness evaluation.

Validity and reliability: Reliability coefficient value of 0.65.

Performance evaluation:

Harvard Step Test	Three Minute test	Rating
<55	0-27	Very Poor.
55-64	28-38	Low average.
65-79	39-48	Average.
80-89	49-59	Good.
-	60-70	Very good
>90	71-100	Excellent.

110

References:

Adams G.M. *Exercise Physiology Laboratory Manual*, Wm C Brown Publishers, Dubuque, 32-39, 1990.

Bandyopadhyay B., Chattopadhyay H. Assessment of physical fitness of sedentary and physically active male college students by a modified Harvard step test. *Journal of Ergonomics*. 24, (1), Jan, 15-20, 1981.

Bonen A. Evaluation of three fitness tests. *Canadian Journal of Public Health*. 66, (4), 228-290, 1975.

Brouha L. The Step Test: A simple method of measuring physical fitness for muscular work in young men. *Research Quarterly*, 14, 31-36, 1943.

Heyward V.H. *Advanced fitness assessment and exercise prescription.* 2nd Edition. Human Kinetics Publishers (UK) Limited, Leeds, 60-61, 1991.

Toriola A.L., Mathur D.N. Relationship between Harvard step test and Cooper's twelve minute run/walk test in determining cardiorespiratory endurance in nonathletic females. *SNIPES Journal*, 9, (2), Apr, 54-57, 1986.

Figure 15.1: Mean PFI values in 10 groups of subjects

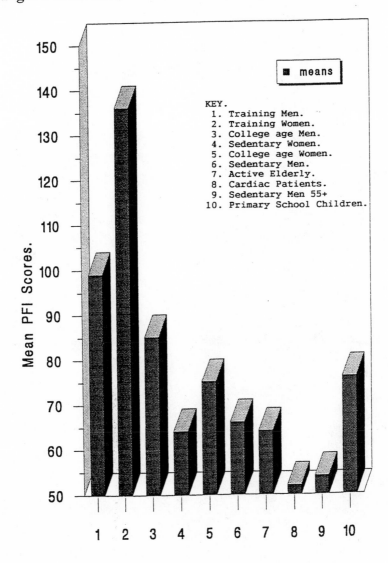

KEY.
1. Training Men.
2. Training Women.
3. College age Men.
4. Sedentary Women.
5. College age Women.
6. Sedentary Men.
7. Active Elderly.
8. Cardiac Patients.
9. Sedentary Men 55+
10. Primary School Children.

CHAPTER 16 : PWC TEST OF PHYSICAL WORKING CAPACITY.

Purpose of test:

To predict the power output at a projected heart rate of 170 beats per minute (P170).

Common usages:

Used to predict aerobic capacity (V_{02} max) based on the belief that heart rate and oxygen uptake are linear functions.

"$V0_2$ max can also provide an insight into the cardio-respiratory system, for example, the clinical severity of disease has been shown to decrease with an increase in functional aerobic capacity". (Bruce et al,1973)

Thus the P170 test can be incorporated into the assessment of cardiovascular and respiratory systems in the transport and diffusion of oxygen.

Equipment :

i) Cycle ergometer; Mechanically braked cycles (e.g. Monark.) are commonly used in laboratories. They produce a constant force but a non constant power at varied pedal revolutions. Therefore, increases in pedal revolutions will alter the work and the power produced.

ii) Stethoscope; Heart rate can be monitored by pulse palpitations, but for greater accuracy a stethoscope can be used. For even more accuracy an electrocardiogram can be used.

iii) Stopwatch; This will be used to measure heart rate.

iv) Laboratory timers; Should be used to measure the duration of the test. If not available then a sweep hand wall clock will suffice.

v) Metronome; To provide a prescribed cadence for the exercising subject. (Adams, 1990)

Procedure: A) *Preparations,*

i) Calibrate the cycle ergometer and metronome.

ii) Measure and record basic physical and meteorological data as temperature or body mass may influence the efficiency of the test.

iii) Familiarise the subject by:
(a) Stating the purpose of the test.

(b) Describe the basic parameters of the test.

(c) Demonstrate cycling cadence.

(d) Gain the subject's permission to perform the test.

iv) Establish and record the height of the seat post for the subject. When the subject is sitting on the cycle with the ball of the foot on the pedal, the leg should have a slight bend of about 155^0 - 160^0. This should illicit a straight leg (180^0) when the subjects heel is on the pedal.

v) Establish the site for auscultation. The heart sound is best heard at the apical region, just below the pectoralis major muscle and left nipple.

vi) Establish the starting power level (kgm.min^{-1} or W) for the protocol (see table 16.1).

B) *Procedure,*

i) Start the metronome.

ii) Ask the subject to begin cycling at the correct cadence.

iii) Once the correct cadence is reached, increase the power level to that prescribed.

iv) As soon as the power level and cadence are

v) Auscultate and time the heart rate between 1 min 30 sec and 2 min. Repeat at intervals described in table 16.1.

vi) Record the 30 second heart beat value on a data sheet.

vii) Calculate beats per minute (times 30 sec value by two) and record on data sheet.

viii) Re-adjust the power level after the 2 min heart rate if heart rate target zone is not reached (see Table 16.2).

ix) If heart rate does not reach target zone after 4th minute then again readjust power level.

x) Record heart rate and power level between 5 min 30 sec and 6 min.

xi) Readjust the power level at the 6th minute to attain the second heart rate target zone, and re-evaluate every two minutes.

xii) Record heart rate and power level between 11 min 30 sec and 12 min.

xiii) Terminate test at 12 minutes and allow the subject to warm down for 3 to 4 minutes at a reduced power level. Monitor heart rate during the warm down.　(Adams, 1990)

Validity and reliability:　A correlation of 0.88 has been reported between P170 and actual V_{02} max (deVries, 1986). A test - retest produced a high reliability of r = 0.88. (deVries & Klafs, 1965)

Special notes:　i) Contraindications to testing should be observed closely at all times.

ii) When in any doubt about safety of testing or health status of the subject, the test must not be performed at that time.

iii) Observations of the condition of the subject, i.e. heart rate and general well being, should be continued for at least four minutes of recovery.

iv) The testing area should be 22^0C (72^0F) or less and the humidity should be 60% or less if possible. (ACSM,1991)

v) Power can be increased either by adding more force or by increasing pedal frequency, as power is a product of the two.

vi) Force and RPM must also be recorded every time heart rate is taken.

Scoring:　There are three methods of scoring in the P170 test;

the nomogram, the graphical and the mathematical method.

1. *Nomogram method*

The nomogram displays the relationship between heart rate (b.min^{-1}) and power (W).

Instructions.

A) Choose on the horizontal axis, the heart rate which corresponds with the power level for the first exercise bout (5½-6 min) and plot on the graph (figure 16.1).

B) Repeat for the second bout of exercise (11½ - 12 min).

C) Place a straight edge ruler between the two points and read the P170 value at the intersect of the straight edge and the vertical axis for the power level. (Ezerski, 1974).

2) *Graphical Method*

A) Choose the power level (horizontal axis) and heart rate (vertical axis) intersect for the first bout of exercise and plot on the graph (figure 16.2).

B) Repeat for the second bout of exercise.

C) Join the two points and extrapolate the line up to a value of 170 BPM.

D) Draw a line perpendicular to the horizontal axis from where the extrapolated line reaches 170 BPM.

E) The intersect of the perpendicular line and the horizontal axis represent the P170 score.

3) *Mathematical method*

This formula is simply derived from the equation for a straight line.

$$P170 = \frac{(P.12 - P.6) \times (170 - HR - 12)}{(HR.12 - HR.6)} + P.12$$

Where: $P.12$ = power level at the 12th minute.

                 $P.6$ = power level at the 6th minute.

                 $HR.12$ = heart rate at the 12th minute.

                 $HR.6$ = heart rate at the 6th minute.

The final score must be expressed relative to body mass. Normal expected values are presented in figures 16.3 to 16.5, with data for figure 16.3 fitted with a third order polynomial, (Adams,1990).

Table 16.1: Protocol for power, target heart rate (HR), and HR time-period for the P170 test in aerobically trained and untrained people.

Time (min:s)		Power	Power	Target HR (b.min^{-1})	HR time-period (min;s)
		untrained	trained		
0.00-6.00	W:	25-100	100-175	120-140	1.30-2.00
	Kgm.min^{-1}:	150-600	600-1050		3.30-4.00
					5.30-6.00
6.00-12.00	W:	75-175	175-250	150-170	7.30-8.00
	Kgm.min^{-1}:	450-1050	1050-1500		9.30-10.00
					11.30-12.00
recovery 12.00-14.00	W:	0-50	50-100	<120	12.30-13.00
	Kgm.min^{-1}:	0-300	300-600		
					13.30-14.00
14.00-16.00				<100	14.30-15.00
					15.30-16.00

(Adams, 1990)

Table 16.2: Power levels at various pedal revolutions (RPM), speeds (kph) and force settings of a mechanically braked cycle ergometer (e.g. Monark).

			Force	(kp;	kg;	X	10	=	N)
			1	2	3	4	5	6	7
RPM	kph		power			(W)	kgm	min^{-1})	
50	18.0	W:	50	100	150	200	250	300	350
		kgm min^{-1}	300	600	900	1200	1500	1800	2100
60	21.6	W:	60	120	180	240	300	360	420
		kgm min^{-1}	360	720	1080	1440	1800	2160	2520

(Adams,1990)

122

References:

Adams F.H., Linde L.M. and Hisazumi M. The physical working capacity of normal school children. *Pediatrics*, 28, 55-65, 1961.

Adams G.M. *Exercise physiology laboratory manual.* California State University, Fullerton, Wm C Brown, 1990.

American College of Sports Medicine. *Guidelines for exercise testing and prescription.* 3rd edition, Philadelphia, Lea & Febiger, 1991.

Bruce R.A., Kusumi F., & Hosmer D. Maximal oxygen intake and nomographic assessment of functional aerobic impairment in cardiovascular disease. *American Heart Journal,* 85, 546-562, 1973.

deVries H.A. & Klafs C.E. Prediction of maximal oxygen intake from submaximal tests. *Journal Of Sports Medicine And Physical Fitness,* 5, 207-214, 1965.

deVries H.A. *Physiology of exercise.* Dubuque, Iowa, Wm C Brown, 1986.

Ezerski V.U. Nomogram for operational calculations of physical work capacity PWC-170.

Yessis Review, 9, (3), 57-59, 1974.

Heyward V.H. *Advanced fitness assessment and exercise prescription.* 2nd Edition. New Mexico, Human Kinetics Books, 1991.

Wahlund H. Determination of the physical working capacity. *Acta Medica Scandinavica,* 132, (suppl. 215), 1-78, 1948.

Watkins J. and Ewing B.G. Physical working capacity and mile run performance in adolescent boys. *British Journal of Sports Medicine*, 17, (3), 188-192, Sept, 1983.

Figure 16.1: P170 nomogram (Ezerski, 1974)

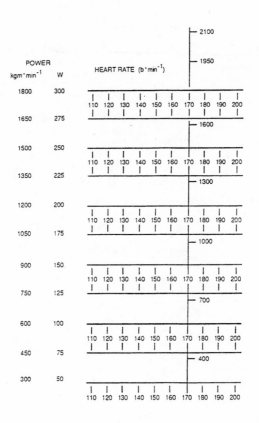

Figure 16.2: An example of graphical calculation of the P-170 test.

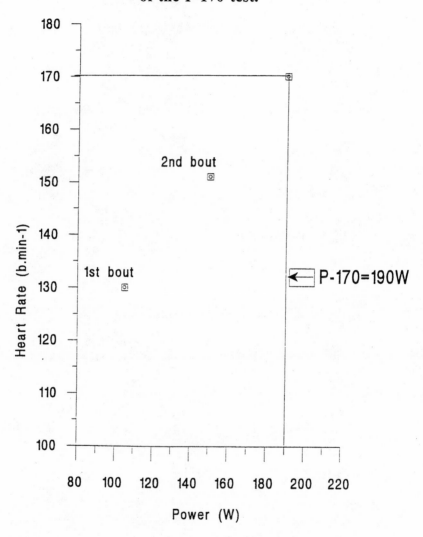

Figure 16.3: Mean norms for P170 scores relative to body mass for males and females aged 7 to 17 (Adams et al, 1961)

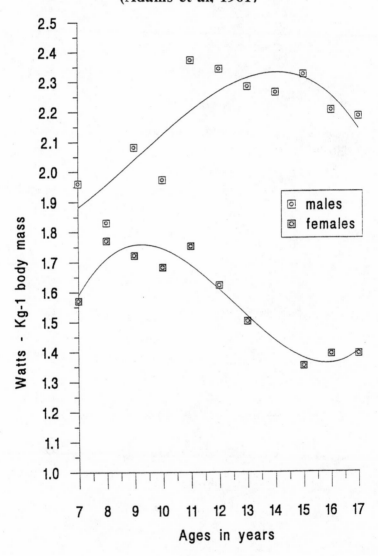

Figure 16.4: Normal values for the P170 test relative
to body mass in males and females aged 18 to 44
(Adams, 1990)

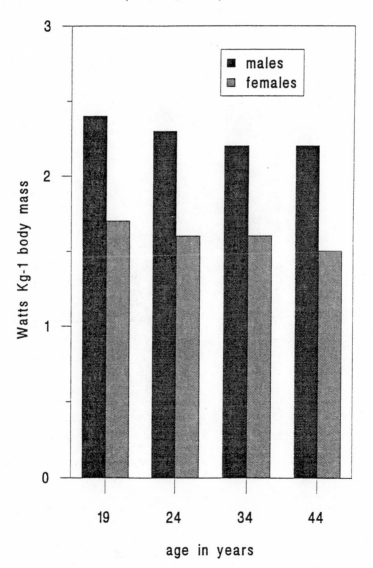

Figure 16.5: Comparison of mean normal data for selected groups of the population (Heyward 1991)

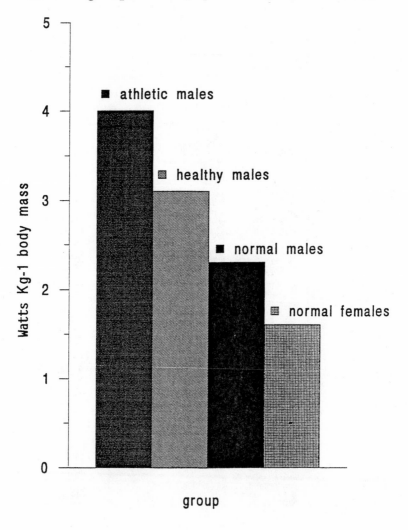

CHAPTER 17 : 20-METRE PROGRESSIVE SHUTTLE RUN TEST (20-MST)

Purpose of test: The 20-MST is a progressive and maximal test of maximum aerobic endurance (VO_2max). It was designed by Léger and Lambert (1982), and is based on the linear relationship between oxygen consumption and running velocity. The 20-MST is currently used in the Eurofit test battery (European test of physical fitness).

Common usages: Whilst results are presented for both males and females between the ages of 6-47 years, the most commonly published results are for adolescents (12-16) and for young adults (18-30). The main use of the 20-MST is in the assessment and monitoring of aerobic fitness in sports performers.

Equipment: - A flat, non-slippery surface at least 20 metres in length

- Cassette player

- Audio cassette (available in the multistage fitness

test)

- Measuring tape to measure the 20 metre track
- Marker cones

Ideally the test is undertaken in a gymnasium or similar hall, with at least one metre clearance beyond each end of the course, and approximately 1 to 1.5 metre wide lanes for each person.

Procedure: The 20-MST consists of 1 minute stages (levels) of continuous running, each at a progressively faster pace. The speed begins at 8.5 $km \cdot h^{-1}$ and increases by 0.5 $km \cdot h^{-1}$ at each successive minute, reaching 18.0 $km \cdot h^{-1}$ at minute 20. Subjects are required to run back and forth between 2 markers spaced 20 m apart, and in time with the bleeps emitted from the tape recorder. Each bleep indicates that the subject should have one foot on or beyond one of the two 20 m markers. If the subject arrives at the end of a shuttle before the bleep sounds, they should turn round and wait for the bleep, then resume running, adjusting their speed. Because the pace of the test increases every minute, but the distance and time remain constant, the number of 20m shuttles (laps) will increase at higher levels. The test ends when the subject stops or fails to get within approximately 3m of an end line on two consecutive occasions. At this point the level, and number of laps into the level which the subject completed should be recorded by an observer. Subjects are asked to complete as many laps as possible up to the point of maximal volitional exhaustion.

Special notes: The 20-MST is easy to administer and suitable for mass testing. It also requires little equipment and can be carried out in a relatively small space either indoors or outdoors making it practical for use in schools without extensive facilities.

Traditional distance runs rely heavily on the ability of subjects to be able to judge pace and to be motivated from the start. These problems are eliminated with the 20-MST since pace is controlled by the audio tape, and the test is incremental and hence submaximal for much of its duration, requiring maximal effort only for the last minute or so. Observers should be present to record the level and number of laps completed by the subject. It is important that subjects both warm-up before the test and cool-down after its completion. The test is progressive and maximal and so should not be undertaken by subjects recovering from illness in the past 10 days, particularly viral infections, or those who suffer from any medical condition that might adversely be effected by severe exercise.

Validity and Reliability: Validity ranges from 0.71 to 0.93, and reliability from 0.89 to 0.97, (Léger and Lambert, 1982., Léger et al, 1988., Lui et al, 1992., Paliczka et al,

1987).

Scoring: The score is taken as the level, and the number of laps into the level, at which the subject withdraws from the test. This score can then be converted into VO_2max using the equations devised by Léger et al (1988).

Children: VO_2max $= 31.025 + 3.238X_1 - 3.248X_2 + 0.1536X_1X_2$

Validity 0.71-0.72   SEE 5.4-5.9 $ml \cdot kg^{-1} \cdot min^{-1}$

(Léger et al, 1988., Lui et al, 1992).

Adults: VO_2max $= -27.4 + 6X_1$

Validity 0.84-0.92   SEE 3.5-5.4 $ml \cdot kg^{-1} \cdot min^{-1}$

(Léger and Lambert, 1982., Léger et al, 1988).

Note, (X_1) speed $km \cdot h^{-1}$, (X_2) age in years, VO_2max expressed in $ml \cdot kg^{-1} \cdot min^{-1}$, (SEE) standard error of estimate.

Table 17.1, is a quick reference chart converting `levels` attained in the shuttle run to predicted VO_2max. However, because this chart does not take account of the number of laps within the final level completed, Tables 17.2A and 17.2B, give a more accurate prediction of VO_2max in adults.

References:

Davis J, (pers comm). *The Lilleshall Human Performance Centre.* Lilleshall National Sports Centre, Newport, Shropshire, 1993.

Eurofit. *European test of physical fitness.* Council of Europe, Committee for the Development of Sport. HMSO, London, 1988.

Hazeldine R., (pers comm). *England Rugby Fitness Advisory Project.* Department of Physical Education, Sport Science and Recreation Management, Loughborough University, 1993.

Léger L.A. and Lambert J. A maximal multistage 20-m shuttle run test to predict VO_2max. *European Journal of Applied Physiology,* 49,1-12, 1982.

Léger L.A., Mercier D., Gadoury C., and Lambert J. The multistage 20 metre shuttle run test for aerobic fitness. *Journal of Sport Sciences,* 6, 93-101, 1988.

Lui N., Plowman S., and Looney M. The reliability and validity of the 20-meter shuttle test in American students 12 to 15 years old. *Research Quarterly for Sport and Exercise,* 63, (4), 360-365, 1992.

Multistage Fitness Test. A progressive shuttle-run test for the prediction of maximal oxygen uptake. National Coaching Foundation, 4 College close, Becket Park, Leeds.

Palickza V.J., Nichols A.K., and Boreham C.A.G. A multi-stage shuttle run as a predictor of running performance and maximal oxygen uptake in adults. *British Journal of Sports Medicine* 21, (4), 163-165, 1987.

Ramsbottom R., Brewer J., and Williams. A progressive shuttle run test to estimate maximal oxygen uptake. *British Journal of Sports Medicine* 22,(4), 141-144, 1988.

Reddin D., (pers comm). Lawn Tennis Association Fitness Test (L.T.A) courtesy of Loughborough University, Department of Physical Education, Sport Science and Recreation Management, 1993.

Table 17.1: Prediction of VO₂max from maximal shuttle run speed and age (Léger et al, 1988).y

Level (min)	Speed (km h⁻¹)	Predicted VO$_2$max (ml·kg^{-1}·min^{-1}) according to speed (km h^{-1}) and age (year)												
		6	7	8	9	10	11	12	13	14	15	16	17	≥18
1	8.5	46.9	45.0	43.0	41.1	39.1	37.2	35.2	33.3	31.4	29.4	27.5	25.5	23.6
2	9.0	49.0	47.1	45.2	43.4	41.5	39.6	37.8	35.9	34.1	32.2	30.3	28.5	26.6
3	9.5	51.1	49.3	47.5	45.7	43.9	42.1	40.3	38.5	36.7	35.0	33.2	31.4	29.6
4	10.0	53.1	51.4	49.7	48.0	46.3	44.6	42.9	41.2	39.4	37.7	36.0	34.3	32.6
5	10.5	55.2	53.6	51.9	50.3	48.7	47.0	45.4	43.8	42.1	40.5	38.9	37.2	35.6
6	11.0	57.3	55.7	54.2	52.6	51.1	49.5	47.9	46.4	44.8	43.3	41.7	40.2	38.6
7	11.5	59.4	57.9	56.4	54.9	53.4	52.0	50.5	49.0	47.5	46.0	44.6	43.1	41.6
8	12.0	61.5	60.1	58.6	57.2	55.8	54.4	53.0	51.6	50.2	48.8	47.4	46.0	44.6
9	12.5	63.5	62.2	60.9	59.6	58.2	56.9	55.6	54.2	52.9	51.6	50.3	48.9	47.6
10	13.0	65.6	64.4	63.1	61.9	60.6	59.4	58.1	56.9	55.6	54.4	53.1	51.9	50.6
11	13.5	67.7	66.5	65.3	64.2	63.0	61.8	60.6	59.5	58.3	57.1	56.0	54.8	53.6
12	14.0	69.8	68.7	67.6	66.5	65.4	64.3	63.2	62.1	61.0	59.9	58.8	57.7	56.6
13	14.5	71.9	70.8	69.8	68.8	67.8	66.8	65.7	64.7	63.7	62.7	61.6	60.6	59.6
14	15.0	73.9	73.0	72.0	71.1	70.2	69.2	68.3	67.3	66.4	65.4	64.5	63.6	62.6
15	15.5	76.0	75.1	74.3	73.4	72.5	71.7	70.8	69.9	69.1	68.2	67.3	66.5	65.6
16	16.0	78.1	77.3	76.5	75.7	74.9	74.1	73.4	72.6	71.8	71.0	70.2	69.4	68.6
17	16.5	80.2	79.5	78.7	78.0	77.3	76.6	75.9	75.2	74.5	73.8	73.0	72.3	71.6
18	17.0	82.3	81.6	81.0	80.3	79.7	79.1	78.4	77.8	77.2	76.5	75.9	75.3	74.6
19	17.5	84.3	83.8	83.2	82.7	82.1	81.5	81.0	80.4	79.9	79.3	78.7	78.2	77.6
20	18.0	86.4	85.9	85.4	85.0	84.5	84.0	83.5	83.0	82.5	82.1	81.6	81.1	80.6

Table 17.2A. Prediction of maximal oxygen uptake values for the progressive shuttle run test (Ramsbottom et al, 1988).

Level	Shuttle	Predicted VO_2max	Level	Shuttle	Predicted VO_2max
4	2	26.8	9	2	43.9
4	4	27.6	9	4	44.5
4	6	28.3	9	6	45.2
4	9	29.5	9	8	45.8
			9	11	46.8
5	2	30.2			
5	4	31.0	10	2	47.4
5	6	31.8	10	4	48.0
5	9	32.9	10	6	48.7
			10	8	49.3
6	2	33.6	10	11	50.2
6	4	34.3			
6	6	35.0	11	2	50.8
6	8	35.7	11	4	51.4
6	10	36.4	11	6	51.9
			11	8	52.5
7	2	37.1	11	10	53.1
7	4	37.8	11	12	53.7
7	6	38.5			
7	8	39.2	12	2	54.3
7	10	39.9	12	4	54.8
			12	6	55.4
8	2	40.5	12	8	56.0
8	4	41.1	12	10	56.5
8	6	41.8	12	12	57.1
8	8	42.4			
8	11	43.3			

Table 17.2B. Prediction of maximal oxygen uptake values for the progressive shuttle run test (Ramsbottom et al, 1988).

Level	Shuttle	Predicted VO_2max	Level	Shuttle	Predicted VO_2max
13	2	57.6	17	2	71.4
13	4	58.2	17	4	71.9
13	6	58.7	17	6	72.4
13	8	59.3	17	8	72.9
13	10	59.8	17	10	73.4
13	13	60.6	17	12	73.9
			17	14	74.4
14	2	61.1			
14	4	61.7	18	2	74.8
14	6	62.2	18	4	75.3
14	8	62.7	18	6	75.8
14	10	63.2	18	8	76.2
14	13	64.0	18	10	76.7
			18	12	77.2
15	2	64.6	18	14	77.9
15	4	65.1			
15	6	65.6	19	2	78.3
15	8	66.2	19	4	78.8
15	10	67.5	19	6	79.2
			19	8	79.7
16	2	68.0	19	10	80.2
16	4	68.5	19	12	80.6
16	6	69.0	19	15	81.3
16	8	69.5			
16	10	69.9	20	2	81.8
16	12	70.5	20	4	82.2
16	14	70.9	20	6	82.6
			20	8	83.0
			20	10	83.5
			20	12	83.9
			20	16	84.8

Figure 17.1: Normal values of a typical (Leger *et al* 1988) and athletic population in the 20-MST (Reddin, 1993)

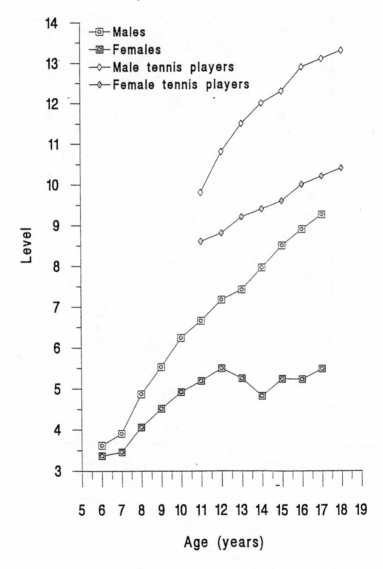

Figure 17.2: Mean values of three male England squads in the 20-MST (Hazeldine, 1993; Davis, 1993)

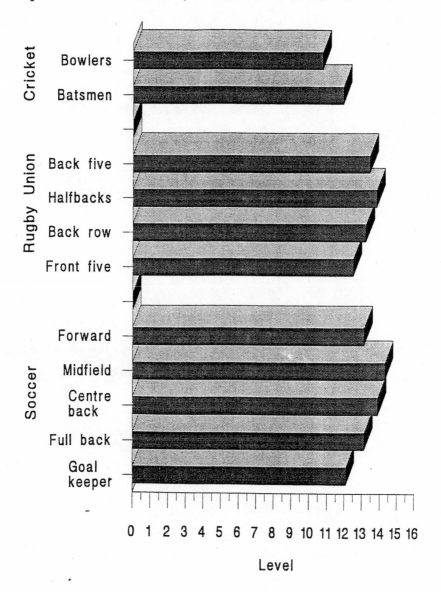

Figure 17.3: Mean values for two female England squads in the 20-MST (Davis, 1993)

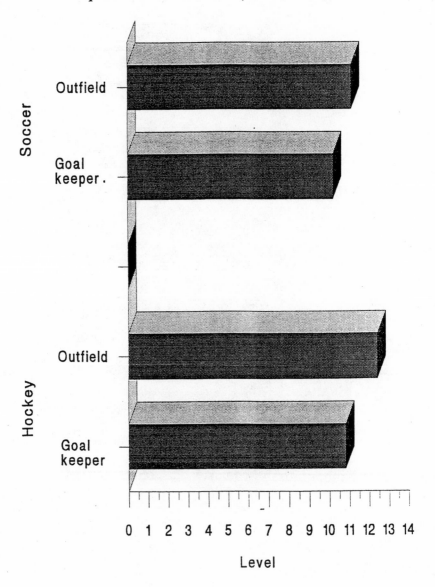

CHAPTER 18 : TWELVE-MINUTE RUN-WALK TEST.

Purpose of test: To evaluate the cardiovascular fitness of individuals by means of a field test.

Common usages: Suitable for measuring large groups of healthy men and women aged 13 and above.

Equipment: Either an indoor/outdoor 400m level track or any other level terrain, accurately measured and marked into subdivisions of 10m; a stopwatch and a whistle.

Procedure: The subjects are instructed to run or jog to cover the longest possible distance in the prescribed duration of 12 minutes. They are informed that a constant, steady pace is more effective but if necessary walking can be adopted. Participants begin on hearing the whistle and continue until the second whistle is sounded at the end of 12 minutes. Subjects are required to count the number of laps they complete. The time elapsed is announced at 9, 11, and 11.5 minute intervals. The subjects are encouraged to increase their pace in the final minute if possible. On hearing the second whistle running is stopped and the distance covered estimated by the runner and technician to the nearest 10m. Values are then compared to normative data tables.

Special notes: This test is a good predictor of aerobic capacity which can be administered to a large group of subjects simultaneously, using a common mode of exercise. It is inexpensive and simple to manage. Use of partners to count laps and estimate total distance reduces error in measurements and eases administration. Cooper (1968) developed a 1.5 mile run test which measures cardiovascular fitness by comparing time to complete the distance with maximal oxygen uptake. This test is easier to administer as lap counting is not required because the distance is set.

Subjects need to warm up thoroughly prior to the test to improve performance and cool down effectively afterwards to limit muscle soreness. All participants should first be screened to remove any with medical conditions which would contraindicate vigorous exercise. Participants should be allowed to practice pacing during distance running to help validate the results. Some subjects will run too fast in the early stages and be forced to slow down or stop due to lactic acid accumulation. Alternatively participants will set off too slowly maintaining this pace throughout. Both of these will produce final performances inappropriate to actual aerobic capacity. Motivation needs to be high because the accuracy of estimating VO_2 max is related directly to motivation of subjects (Cooper 1968). Other factors which effect running performance apart from aerobic capacity are body mass, percentage fat mass, technique and running efficiency plus percentage of aerobic capacity which can be sustained without a detrimental build up of lactic acid. Caution is therefore necessary when estimating Vo_2 max directly from endurance run tests due to these variables.

Validity and Reliability: Reliability by test-retest method has produced coefficients of 0.75 (Gunn et al, 1976) to 0.94 (Doolittle and Bigbee, 1968). Validity coefficients for oxygen consumption and field test data are reported to range from 0.34 (Jessup et al, 1973) to 0.9 (Doolittle and Bigbee, 1968). Cooper (1968) reported a correlation of 0.89 using US Air Force male officers (n=115) of 17-52 years of age. Few researchers have been able to obtain this high validity coefficient. This variability may be attributed to the samples studied, for most used relatively homogenous groups with a small sample size. Whereas Cooper's original sample was heterogenous and large. These results reveal Coopers 12-minute run-walk test to be highly

144

reliable and a valid indicator of oxygen intake, an accepted measure of cardiovascular fitness, in large heterogenous samples.

Scoring: The score is the distance covered in 12 minutes to the nearest 10m.

References: American Alliance for Health, Physical Education, Recreation, and Dance. *Health-related physical fitness test manual.* Washington, DC, 1980.

Cooper K.H. (1977) A means of assessing maximum oxygen intake. In Bosco J.S., and Gustafson W.F. *Measurement and Evaluation in Physical Education Fitness and Sport.* Pentice-Hall inc, Englewood Cliffs, New Jersey, 1983.

Cooper K.H. A means of assessing maximal oxygen intake, correlation between field and treadmill testing. *Journal of the American Medical Association,* 203, (3), 135-138, 1968.

Cooper K.H. Testing and developing cardiovascular fitness within the United States Air Force. *Journal of Occupational Medicine,* 10, (11), 636-639, 1968.

Doolittle T.L., and Bigbee R. The twelve minute run-walk: A test of cardiorespiratory fitness of adolescent boys. *Research Quarterly,* 39, (3), 491-

495, 1968.

Gunn B., Fogle R.K., and Stewart K. Relationship among submaximal heart rate and aerobic power and running performance in children. *Research Quarterly*, 47, (4), 536-539, 1976.

Jackson A.S., and Coleman A.E. Validation of distance run tests for elementary school children. *Research Quarterly*, 47, (1), 86-94, 1976.

Jessup G.T., et al. Prediction of maximal oxygen intake from Astrand-Rhyming test, 12-minute run and anthropometric variables using stepwise multiple regression. *Research Paper Presented at the 1973 AAHPER Convention*, Minneapolis, 1973.

Figure 18.1: Normal values for men from the twelve-minute run-walk test. Source of data, Cooper (1977)

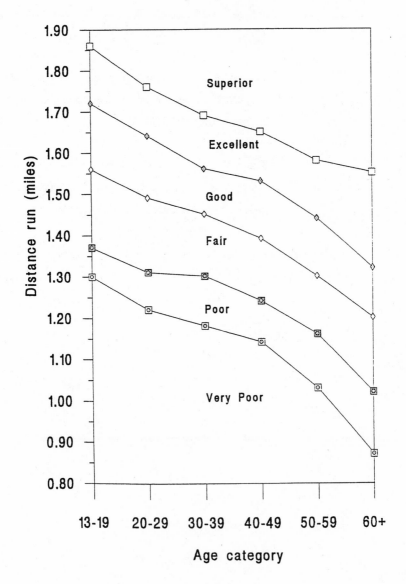

Figure 18.2: Normal values for women from the twelve-minute run-walk test. Source of data, Cooper (1977)

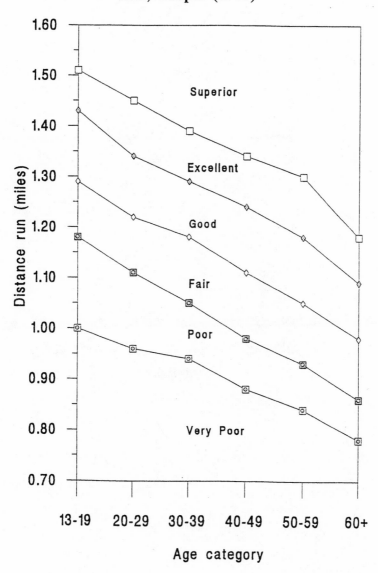

CHAPTER 19 : AAHPERD 9-MINUTE RUN TEST

Purpose of test: To measure cardiovascular endurance by an objective field test.

Common usages: Recommended for boys and girls aged 5-12, also suitable for college students if preferred.

Equipment: A 400m flat track or any other accurately measured level terrain marked into subdivisions of 10m, a whistle and a stopwatch.

Procedure: Administration of this test follows the same structure as the aforementioned 12-minute run-walk test, although the duration is reduced to 9 minutes and time elapsed is announced at 8 and 8.5 minutes.

Special notes: This test is practical, simple and inexpensive to administer to a large group of school children in a relatively short time period, e.g. 15 minutes. All students should be thoroughly warmed up before starting the test and be given taper down activities afterwards. No child should be allowed to participate who is known to have a medical condition which will be aggravated by vigorous exercise. Strong emphasis on pacing is needed for young children have problems understanding the concept unless they run regularly. Motivation is a problem as reported by Safrit and Wood (1987) who noted that in some cases the children refused to run and walked for the entire time. Very young children might also have difficulty keeping count of the laps completed and others may forget to refrain from eating beforehand, producing artificial results. To improve the accuracy partners can be used to count the laps or an alternative 1 mile run test (AAHPERD 1984) can be administered, where time is the variable.

Validity and Reliability: The 9-minute run test is reliable in measuring running ability in young children. Coefficients range from 0.43-0.71 for boys and 0.58-0.82 for girls (Safrit and Wood, 1987). This test is also a valid measure of cardiovascular endurance with correlations between distance run and max Vo_2 being as high as 0.82 for boys and 0.77 for girls (Jackson and Coleman, 1976).

Scoring: The score is the distance covered in the duration of 9-minutes to the nearest 10m.

References: AAHPERD. *Norms for College Students.* Washington, DC, 1985.

AAHPERD. *Health-Related Physical Fitness Test Technical Manual*. Washington, DC, 1984.

Balke B. A simple field test for the assessment of physical fitness. *Civil Aeromedical Research Institute. Federal Aviation Agency, CARI Report*, 63-78, 1963.

Jackson A.S., and Coleman A.E. Validation of distance run tests for elementary school children. *Research quarterly*, 47, (1), 86-94, 1976.

Safrit M.J., and Wood T.M. The test battery reliability of health-related physical fitness test. *Research Quarterly for Exercise and Sport*, 58, (2), 160-167, 1987.

Figure 19.1: Percentile values for women from
the AAHPERD 9-minute run test. Source of data,
Jackson and Coleman (1976).

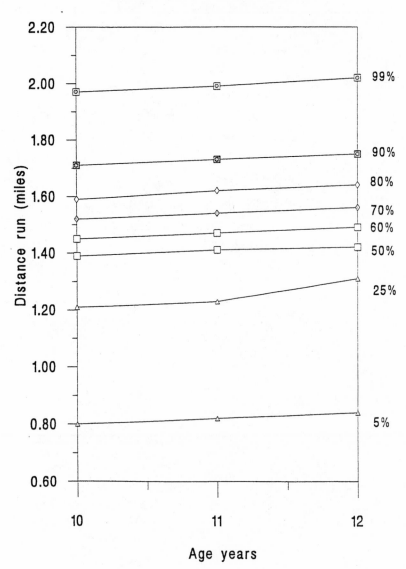

Figure 19.2: Percentile values for men from the AAHPERD 9-minute run test. Source of data, Jackson and Coleman (1976)

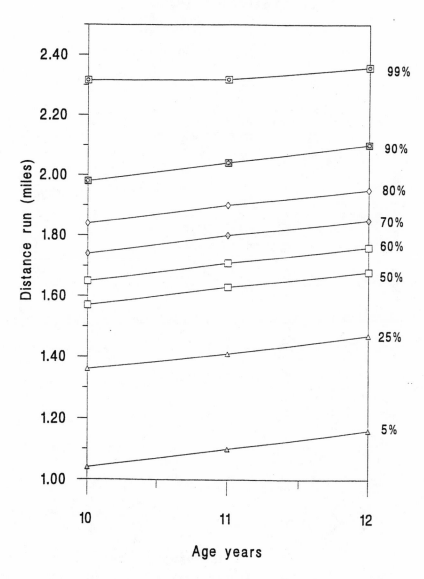

Figure 19.3: Percentile values for women from the AAHPERD 9-minute run test. Source of data, AAHPERD (1985)

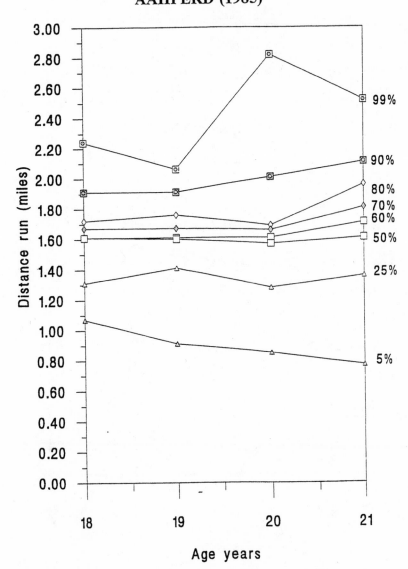

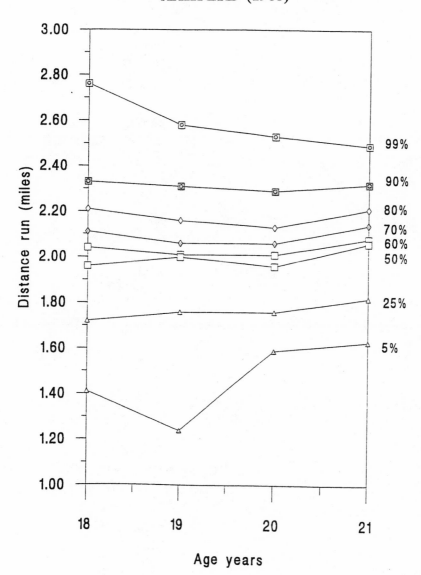

Figure 19.4: Percentile values for men from the
AAHPERD 9-minute run test. Source of data,
AAHPERD (1985)

CHAPTER 20 : MODIFIED SIT-UPS

Purpose of Test: To measure abdominal strength and endurance.

Common usages: Results are available for males and females (aged six upwards).

Equipment: The only equipment required is a mat and a stopwatch.

Procedure: The subject lies on the back with feet on the floor, knees flexed, and heels between 30cm to 45cm from the buttocks. The arms are crossed on the chest with the hands on the opposite shoulder. The feet are held by a partner to keep them in touch with the testing surface. The subject begins tightening the abdominal muscles and curls to the sitting position. Arm contact with the chest must be maintained, chin remains tucked on the chest when the elbows touch the thighs. The sit-up is completed when the student returns down to a position where the midback makes contact with the testing surface.

The examinee begins executing consecutive sit-ups on the word "Go!", using the signal "Ready Go!" Performance is stopped 60 seconds later on the word "Stop!" The examiner counts the number of correctly executed sit-ups during the time period.

Scoring: The score is the number of correctly executed sit-ups in 60 seconds.

Special notes: The subject should be aware that rest is allowed between sit-ups and should breathe early during the exercise so as not to involve the valsalva manoeuvre. Incorrect execution includes failure to curl up, pulling the arms away from the chest, failure to touch the thighs with the elbows, and failure to touch the testing surface with the midback in the down position.

Reliability: The reliability of this test is generally satisfactory with test-retest reliability coefficients as high as 0.94.

Validity: There have been few attempts to validate sit-ups against larger batteries of muscular tests. Electromyographic studies have shown the abdominal muscles are active during sit-ups, although no evidence exists that a specified number of sit-ups reflects a desirable amount of abdominal strength and endurance. Thus the modified sit-up is validated on the basis of logical or content validity.

Comments: Interpretive error for this test will result most often from the individuals failure to execute the sit-up correctly. Lack of validity may be due simply to the fact that the sit-up test is usually correlated against tests of the arms and shoulder girdle and that the endurance of the abdominals simply does not correlate highly with the endurance of the muscles of the arms and shoulder girdle.

Reference: American Association for Health, Physical Education, Recreation and Dance. *Health-related physical fitness test manual*, AAHPERD, Virginia, 1984.

Figure 20.1: Modified sit-ups percentile norms
for females (AAPHERD, 1984)

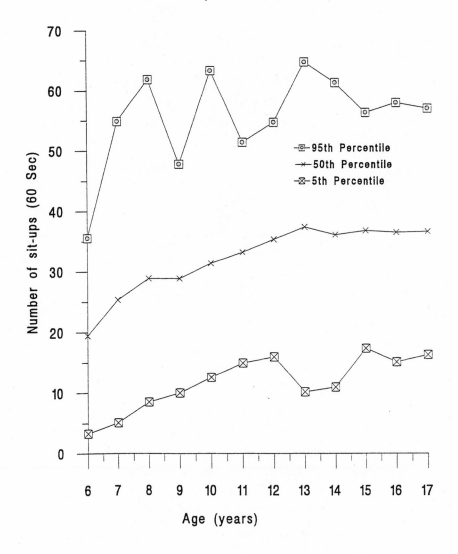

Figure 20.2: Modified sit-ups percentile norms for males (AAPHERD, 1984)

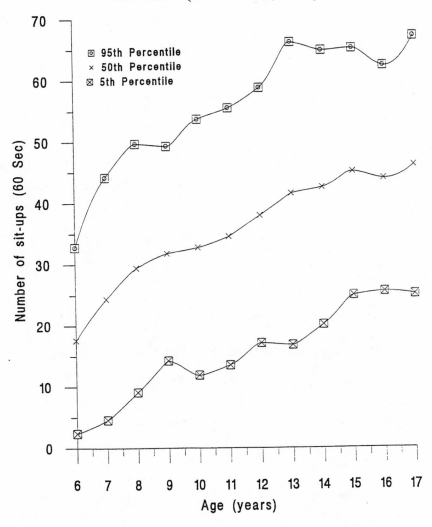

CHAPTER 21 : PULL-UP TEST

Purpose of test: To measure the muscular endurance of the arms and shoulder girdle in pulling the body upward.

Common usages: Most results are presented for males only (aged 9 upwards) but a modified pull-up can be used for younger children of both sexes.

Equipment: Horizontal bar 3.8cm (1.5in) in diameter raised to a height so that the tallest subject cannot touch the ground from the hanging position.

Procedure: The subject should hang from the horizontal bar using the overhand grasp, palms forward. The hands are at shoulder width and feet clear of the floor. On the signal "Go!" the subject raises his/her body using the arms until the chin is above the level of the bar and without delay should return to the fully extended position. The procedure should be repeated as many times as possible. The test is terminated if the subject (1) stops to rest, (2) performs a swinging motion or flexes the knees, (3) the chin does not rise above the horizontal bar, or (4) the arms are not fully extended during the hanging phase.

Special notes: Each subject is allowed one trial. No advantage can be gained by swinging or kicking the legs. This can be checked by the administrator holding an outstretched arm across the thighs. The modified pull- up test differs in that (1) The bar is lowered to the height of chest, (2) the heels touch the floor, and (3) the subject extends the arms to allow the chin to rise above the bar. Warn the subjects about the potential danger of hitting their chin on the bar when they tire.

Scoring: The score is the total number of correctly executed pull-ups.

Validity and Reliability: The test has been accepted for its construct validity of the basic component muscular strength of the arms and shoulder girdle involved in moving the body weight. Reliability of 0.87 reported.

References: American Association for Health, Physical Education, Recreation and Dance. *Health-related physical fitness test manual*, AAHPERD, Virginia, 1980

Johnson B.L. and Nelson J.K. *Practical*

measurements for evaluation in physical education, 3rd Edition, Burgess Publishing Company, Minneapolis, Minnesota, 124-125, 1979.

Campbell W.R., and Tucker N.M. *An introduction to tests and measurements in physical education.* Bell, London, 1967.

Figure 21.1: Bar chart showing percentile rank norms for pull-ups (males).

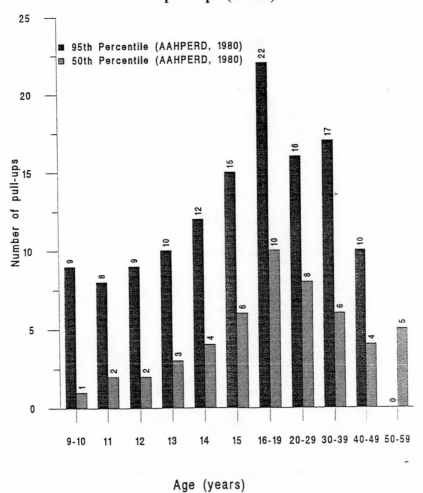

Figure 21.2: Modified pull-ups percentile norms for British girls (AAHPERD, 1980)

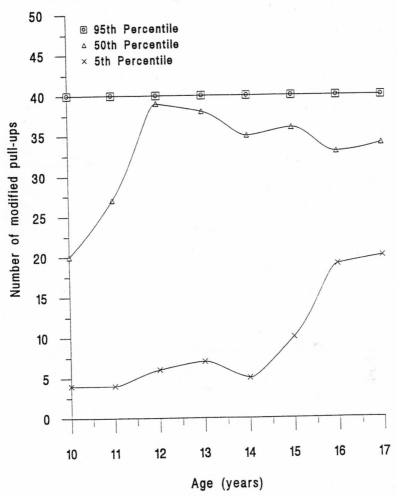

CHAPTER 22 : FLEXED ARM HANG

Purpose of test: To measure the local muscular endurance of the arms and shoulder girdle.

Common Usages: Most results are presented for females only (aged 9-17). Test can be used for males who cannot perform pull-ups and for younger children (5-9) of both sexes.

Equipment: Horizontal bar 3.8cm (1.5in) in diameter raised to a height so that the tallest subject cannot touch the ground from the flexed arm-hang position. Stopwatch.

Procedure: The subject uses an overhand grasp, palms forward. Assisted by two spotters, one in front and one at the back, the subject raises the body off the floor to a position where the chin is above the bar, the elbows are flexed, and the chest is close to the bar. Start stopwatch when the subject reaches the hanging position. Stop the watch when (1) the subject's chin touches the bar, (2) the subject's head tilts backwards to keep the chin above the bar, or (3) the subject's chin falls below the level of the bar.

Special notes: Spotters are important as subjects can lose their grip and fall. Warn subjects about the potential danger of hitting their chin on the bar when they tire. In a 45-minute period a class of 50 students can be tested. The Texas Test (1973) is an alternative procedure and is identical to the one described above except (1) the palms are reversed facing the subject and (2) the test ends after the subject maintains the proper positions for 90 seconds.

Scoring: The score is the number of seconds to the nearest second that the subject maintains the hanging position.

Validity and reliability: Face validity accepted. Reliability as high as 0.90 reported.

References: American Association for Health, Physical Education, Recreation and Dance. *Youth fitness test manual*, Revised Edition, AAHPERD, Washington, D.C., 1976.

American Association for Health, Physical Education, Recreation and Dance. *Health-related physical fitness test manual*, AAHPERD, Virginia, 1980.

Gabbard C., Patterson P. and Elledge J. Effects of grip and forearm position on flexed-arm hang performance. *Research Quarterly for Exercise and Sports*, 54, (2), 198-199, 1983.

Kemper H.C.G., and Verschuur R. Motor Performance fitness tests. In, Kemper, H.C.G. (Ed.), Growth, Health Fitness of Teenagers. (Chap. 11). *Medicine and Science in Sports Exercise*, (20), 96-106.

Texas Governor's Commission on Physical Fitness, *Physical fitness motor ability test*, Austin, TX, 1973.

Figure 22.1: Normal values for flexed-arm hang

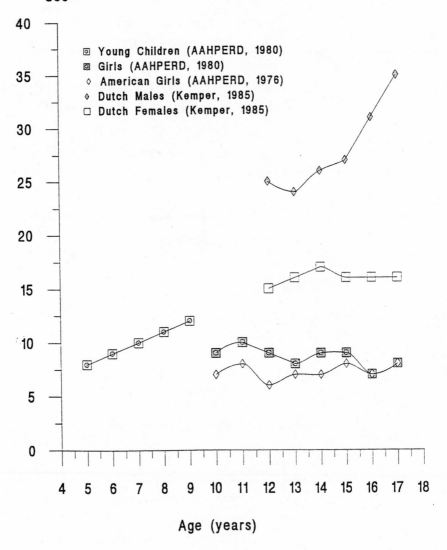

Sec

Young Children (AAHPERD, 1980)
Girls (AAHPERD, 1980)
American Girls (AAHPERD, 1976)
Dutch Males (Kemper, 1985)
Dutch Females (Kemper, 1985)

Age (years)

CHAPTER 23 : 50 YARD DASH

Purpose of test: To measure speed, explosive strength and to calculate anaerobic power.

Common usages: Most results are reported for children of both sexes but the test can be used for subjects of any age.

Equipment: Sufficient floor space to mark out a 50yd course. Chalk to mark the 2 parallel lines. Stopwatch accurate to one tenth of a second.

Procedure: The subject assumes a standing start position behind the first restraining line. Using a "Go!" signal, the test is started. The subject runs as fast as possible without slowing down until crossing the finish line.

Special notes: This test can be performed either inside or outside although if outside conditions must be calm - i.e. very little wind and dry. In recent years cycle ergometer tests have replaced the classic techniques for anaerobic power and traditional field testing such as vertical jump, standing broad jump and the 50yd dash. The most popular cycle ergometer test for anaerobic power is the Wingate test described in chapter 12. The correlation between the 50yd dash and the Wingate test is r=0.66.

Validity and Reliability: Validity as high as 0.9 has been reported and a reliability of 0.95.

Scoring: The score is the time taken to the nearest one tenth of a second to run the 50yd distance.

References: AAHPER, *Youth and Fitness test manual.* Washington D.C. AAHPER, 1976.

Tharp G.D. et al. Comparison of sprint times with performance of the Wingate anaerobic test. *Research Quarterly* 56, (1), p.73, 1985.

Campbell W.R. and Rohndorf R.H. Physical Fitness in British and US children. *Health and Fitness in the Modern World*, p.8-16, 1967.

Fleishman E.A. *The structure and measurement of physical fitness.* Prentice Hall, Englewood Cliffs, 1964

MacDougall J.D., Wenger H.A., Green H.J. *Physiological testing of the elite athlete.* Canadian association of sports sciences. Sports Medicine Council of Canada, 1982.

Figure 23.1: 50th percentile for 50 yard dash times

for males

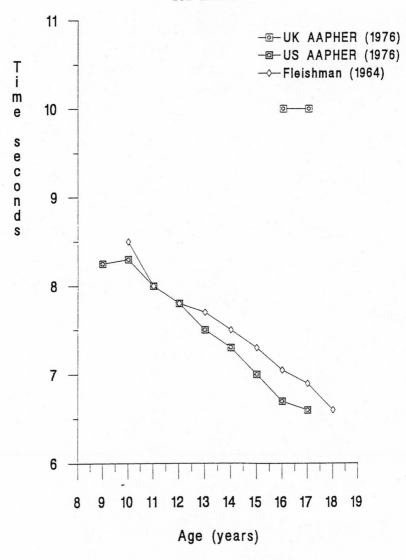

Figure 23.2: 50th percentile for 50 yard dash times for females

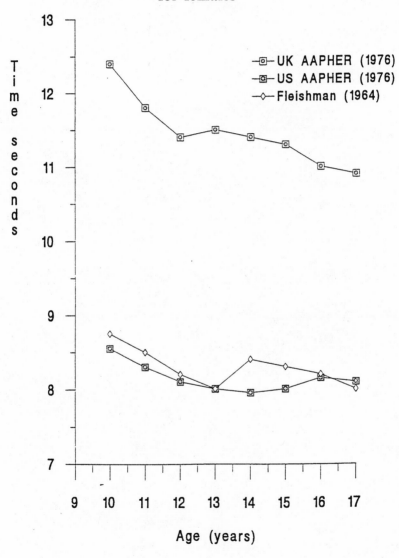

CHAPTER 24 : SHUTTLE RUN

Purpose of test:

To measure speed, change of direction, explosive leg strength and running agility.

Common usages:

Most results are presented for both sexes (aged 9 - 17 years) but the test can be used with collegiate or indeed other subjects.

Equipment:

Sufficient floor space to measure out a course of 30ft. Stopwatch accurate to one tenth of a second. Chalk and 2 wooden blocks per test station.

Procedure:

Chalk 2 parallel lines on the floor, 30ft apart. Place the 2 wooden blocks behind one of the lines. The subject starts from behind the other line. The test is started by a "Go!" signal and a down stroke of the arm. The subject runs to the blocks, picks one up and runs back to the start line placing it on the floor. The subject then repeats this collecting the second block as fast as fast as possible.

Special notes: Fleishman (1964) used parallel lines 20yds apart; the subject completing 5 trips. Cooper (1963) used lines 30ft apart and 10 trips were completed.

Validity and Reliability: Validity as high as 0.9 has been reported. Reliability as high as 0.97 has been reported.

Scoring: The score is the time taken to the nearest tenth of a second, for the subject to complete the course.

References: AAHPER *Youth and Fitness Test Manual.* Washington D.C. AAHPER, 1976.

Campbell W.R. and Rohndorf R.H. Physical fitness in British and US Children. *Health and Fitness in the Modern World,* p.8-16, 1967.

Cooper D.M., Weiler-Ravel D., Whipp B.J., Wasserman K. Aerobic parameters of exercise as a function of body size during growth in children. *Journal of Applied Physiology,* 56, p.628-634, 1984

Cooper K.H. A means of assessing max O2 uptake. *Journal of American Medical Association*, 203, p.201-204, 1963.

Fleishman E.A. *The structure and measurement of physical fitness*. Prentice Hall, Englewood Cliffs, 1964.

Larson C.A. *Fitness, Health and Work Capacity*. International standards for assessment, 1974.

Figure 24.1: 50th percentile times of shuttle runs
for males

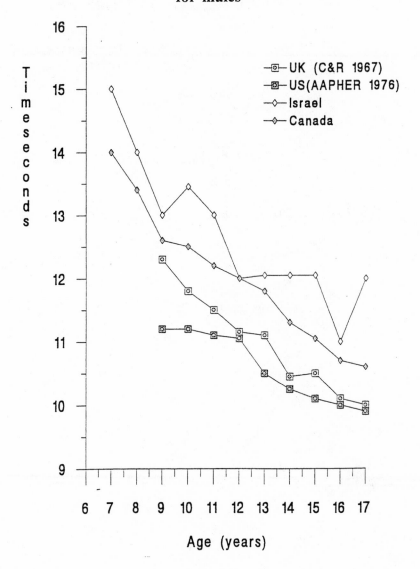

Figure 24.2: 50th percentile times of shuttle runs
for females

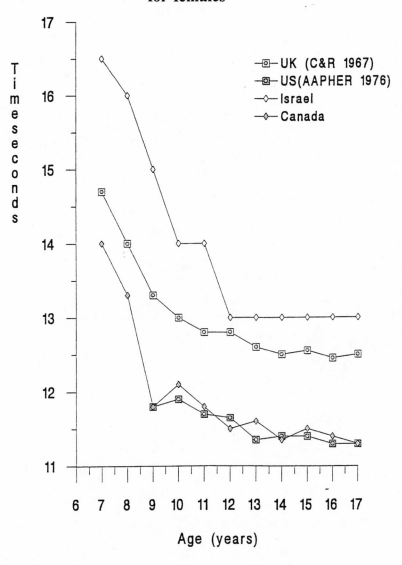

CHAPTER 25 : AAPHER YOUTH FITNESS TEST.

Introduction.

The Youth fitness test was first introduced in 1956 when it was established that American children fared poorly in comparison with European children in tests of minimal muscular fitness. (Kraus and Hirschland, 1954.) The test items were as follows:

1) **Pull-ups**: To measure arm and shoulder girdle strength.

2) **Sit-ups**: To measure the efficiency of the abdominal and hip flexor muscles,

3) **Shuttle run**: For speed and agility,

4) **Standing long jump**: To measure the explosive muscular power of the leg extensors,

5) **50 yard dash**: Measure of speed,

6) **600 yard run/walk**: To measure cardiovascular efficiency and

7) **Softball throw**: Indication of sporting skills.

The test was revised between 1958 and 1975 when several changes were made. The flexed arm hang was substituted for the modified pull-ups for girls; the softball throw for distance was deleted, and the sit-up was changed from an extended leg sit-up with a maximum number of 100 for boys and 50 for girls, to a one-minute sit-up with the knees flexed. In 1976, optional distance runs of 9 minutes or 1 mile for ages 10-12 and 12 minutes or 1.5 miles for ages 13 and over were included because empirical evidence had shown these to be a better predictor of cardiorespiratory endurance than the 600 yard run/walk.

Each test item is viewed as an indicator of a strength or weakness on a specific component of fitness. There is little interest in the total test score.

The tests can easily be administered by mass testing with partners for the sit-ups and 600 yard run. The other tests can be tested using stations with a trained tester at each station. For a group of 30 to 35 subjects the test can be completed in two 45 minute periods. Pull-ups, flexed arm hangs, sit-ups, standing long jump and shuttle runs in the first period and the 50 yard dash and distance runs in the second period. With good organisation the test can be administered in reasonable time.

The test is safe if carried out as indicated, but a warm-up is emphasized to reduce injury risk.

The AAPHER Youth fitness test is aimed to measure the status and achievement in physical fitness of youths, aged 9-17. The original norms were established for all six parameters from a sample of 8500 boys and girls selected from schools by the Survey Research Centre of the University of Michigan in 1958. These were then updated in 1965 and 1976.

Individual test descriptions are present on the following pages.

References: *AAPHERD Health related physical fitness manual.* Reston, VA, AAHPER, 1980.

Hunisicker P. and Rieff G. *AAPHER youth fitness test manual.* (Revised edition) Washington, DC, AAPHER, 1976.

Kraus H. and Hirschland R.P. Minimum muscular fitness tests in school children. *Research Quarterly*, 255, 178-188, 1954.

188

Test Descriptions.

Test 1: Pull-ups/Flexed arm hang.

For test descriptions and scoring, refer to Chapters 21 and 22 respectively.

Test 2: Sit-ups.

For test description and scoring, refer to Chapter 20.

Test 3: Shuttle run.

For test description and scoring, refer to Chapter 24.

Test 4: 50 Yard dash.

For test description and scoring, refer to Chapter 23.

Test 5: 600 Yard run/walk.

Purpose: To measure cardiorespiratory endurance.

Common usages: Results are presented for both males and females, ages 9-17+ years.

Equipment: Running track, school field or square 50 yards each side. Stopwatch.

Procedure: Subjects use a standing start. At the signal "Ready?, Go!" subject begins running the 600 yard distance. Running may be interspersed with walking if subject unable to run the whole distance.

As subject passes the finish line, the time is recorded.

Special notes: Subjects should run together in groups to allow mass testing to be feasible. The course should be in the form of a circuit to prevent subjects having to slow down unnecessarily. Alternative procedures are the 1 mile or 9 minute run test. Safrit (1986) reported that the longer the run, the higher the correlations with maximal oxygen consumption. Therefore these tests are a more valid measure of aerobic power.

Validity and Reliability: Correlations between the 600 yard run time and a measure of maximal oxygen consumption ranged from -0.27 to -0.71. Reliability is high ranging from 0.65 to 0.92.

Scoring: Time is recorded in minutes and seconds.

References: *AAHPER, Youth fitness test manual*, Washington DC, AAHPER, 1976.

AAHPERD, Health related fitness manual. Reston, VA, AAHPER, 1980.

Safrit H.M. *Introduction to measurement in physical education and exercise science.* Times Mirror/Mosby College Publishing, 263-297, 1986.

Figure 25.1: 600 Yard Run

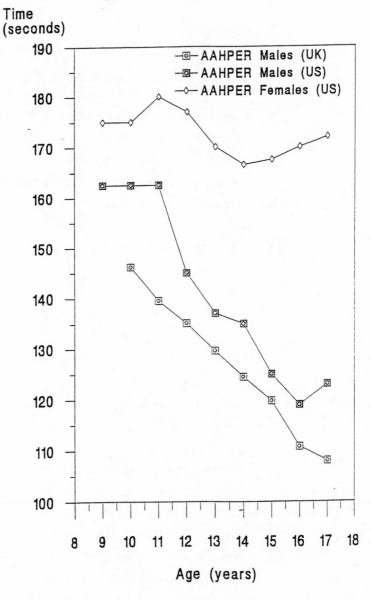

CHAPTER 26 : AAPHERD HEALTH-RELATED FITNESS TEST.

Introduction.

During the 1970's a major philosophical influence changed the focus of fitness testing. It changed from the assessment of athletic performance to that of health related performance (Barrow *et al*, 1989). This was thought to offer the individual some degree of protection against degenerative diseases such as coronary heart disease, obesity and musculoskeletal disorders.

The Health Related Physical Fitness Test (HRPFT) was first published in 1980. This was devised as a revision of the already existing Youth Fitness Test (first published in 1957) because it was thought that this did not place sufficient emphasis upon the health related aspects of physical performance. Since physical fitness can be operationally defined by the test items used for its evaluation, each test first had to satisfy specific criteria. These were:

1) A physical fitness test should measure a range which extends from severely limiting dysfunction to high levels of functional capacity;

2) It should measure capacities that can be improved with appropriate physical activity; and

3) It should accurately reflect an individual's physical fitness status as well as changes in functional capacity by corresponding test scores and changes in these scores.

The HRPFT contains the recommended fundamental components of health related fitness along with suggested test items (AAPHERD, 1984). They were selected because they all met the above criteria. These included:

Fitness Component	*Recommended Test Item(s)*
1) Cardiorespiratory fitness	Mile run/walk, or 9 min run walk
2) Body composition	Triceps and subscapular skinfolds
3) Abdominal and low back musculoskeletal function	Timed sit-ups and sit and reach.

Cardiorespiratory fitness (CRF) can be justified as an important component of physical fitness since it is related to health and is affected by physical activity. Decreased levels of CRF increase the possibility of cardiovascular disease. This has reached epidemic proportions in most industrialised countries. The American Heart Association estimates that ten years ago there were some 600,000 deaths in the USA through CHD alone. (AAPHERD, 1984.)

The measurement of body composition is important because it has been estimated that 33% of the American population is obese. (AAPHERD, 1984.) There is a relationship between obesity and CHD, hypertension and depression.

The maintenance of good abdominal strength/endurance and low back/hamstring flexibility decreases the risk of developing low back pain. This accounts for more lost manhours than any other injury costing over one billion dollars in lost productivity *per annum*. (Amudsen, 1973.)

For all of the above tests, percentile norms exist. These were taken from national surveys (1979) of over 12,000 boys and girls ranging in age from 6-17 years.

Test scores can be a significant aid in the prescription of exercise for the development of physical fitness. Attained scores on the various test items can be used to identify strengths and weaknesses within individual subjects and also to determine the degree to which the test objectives are being met.

Descriptions of the individual items of the HRPFT are presented on the following pages.

References:

AAPHERD, Health related physical fitness technical manual, Reston, VA, AAHPER, 1984.

AAPHERD, Health related physical fitness test manual, Reston, VA, AAPHER, 1980.

Amudsen M.A. A look at the back, a clinical view. *Occupational Health Nursing*, 21, 21-24, 1973.

Barrow H.M, McGee R. and Tritschler K.A. *A practical measurement in physical education and sport*. Lea and Febiger, Philadelphia, 1989.

Cardiorespiratory Fitness. (Distance runs).

For description and scoring of the one mile/9 minute run/walk refer to Chapter 19.

Body Composition. (Sum of skinfold fat).

Purpose of test:	To evaluate the level of fatness in school age boys and girls from the sum of the triceps and subscapular skinfolds.
Common Usages:	Results are presented for both males and females, age range 6-18 years and 18-21 years.
Equipment:	The Harpenden (Quinton Instrument Company, Seattle WA) and Lange (Cambridge Scientific Industries, MD) skinfold callipers are recommended. The characteristics of these include accurate calibration capability and a constant pressure of 10 $gm.mm^{-2}$ throughout the range of skinfold thickness.
Procedure:	*Triceps*: Skinfold measured over the triceps muscle of the right arm halfway between the elbow and the acromion process of the scapular with the skinfold parallel to the longitudinal axis of the upper arm.
	Subscapular: Skinfold taken on the right hand side

of the body 1cm below the inferior angle of the scapula in line with the natural cleavage lines of the skin.

The recommended testing procedure is:

1) Firmly grasp the skinfold between the thumb and forefinger and lift up.

2) Place the contact surfaces of the calliper 1cm above or below the finger.

3) Slowly release the grip on the callipers enabling them to exert their full tension on the skinfold.

4) Read skinfold to the nearest 0.5mm after needle stops (1 to 2 seconds after releasing grip on the calliper).

Special notes: When measuring the subscapular skinfold in females, it is recommended that the individual being tested wear a loose fitting T-shirt or similar garment. The shirt can be raised at the back to allow access to the skinfold site.

Do not place the callipers at the base of the skinfold. This will only give a reading that does not reflect the true thickness and will be too large.

It is recommended that the same tester administer

the skinfold fat test on the same subjects on subsequent testing periods. Inter-tester error is common and may make the interpretation of subsequent measurements confusing and misleading. Although the recommended procedure is the sum of the two skinfolds, if it is only possible to secure just one skinfold, then the triceps should be the selected site.

Validity and Reliability: Validity co-efficients between skinfolds and hydrostatically determined body fatness have consistently ranged from 0.70 to 0.90 in both children and adults. (Baumgartner and Jackson, 1982.)

Test-retest reliability is high. Adams (1990) retested 28 subjects after a 24 hour period and found a test-retest correlation of $r = 0.96$.

Scoring: The skinfold measurement is registered on the dial of the calliper. Each measurement should be taken three times. The recorded score is the median of the three scores. Each reading should be recorded to the nearest 0.5 mm.

References: *AAPHERD, Health related physical fitness test manual*, Reston, VA, AAHPER, 1980.

Adams G.M. *Exercise physiology laboratory*

manual. Wm.C.Brown Publishers, 1990.

Baumgartner T.A. and Jackson A.S. *Measurement for evaluation in physical education*, 2nd ed. Houghton Mifflin, Boston, 1982.

Johnston F.E., Hamill D.V. and Lemeshow, S. *1) Skinfold thicknesses of children, 6-11 years* (Series II, No.120, 1972) and *2) Skinfold thicknesses of youths, 12-17 years* (Series II, No.132, 1974). US National Centre for Health Statistics, US Department of HEW, Washington DC.

Abdominal and low back musculoskeletal function.

Sit and reach.

For description and scoring of the sit and reach test refer to Chapter 6.

Sit-ups.

For description and scoring of the sit-up test refer to Chapter 20.

Figure 26.1: Sum of skinfold measures

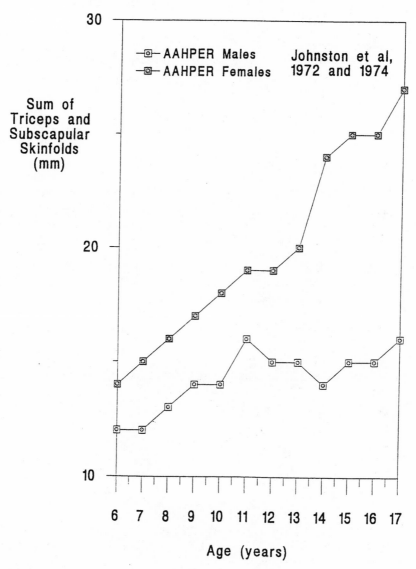

CHAPTER 27 : THE EUROPEAN TEST OF PHYSICAL FITNESS (EUROFIT)

Introduction:

The purpose of this test is to provide an effective means of accurately assessing physical fitness in children, aged from six to eighteen, appropriate to school and survey use. The Eurofit tests are designed to measure a child's progress in the development of their basic physical attributes.

The need for testing physical fitness and the establishment of reference for European school children was first recognised in 1977 at the meetings of the Directors of Sports Research Institutes. The project's principal aims were;

1) to establish a commonly agreed test battery in Europe;

2) to help teachers in assessing the physical fitness of their pupils in schools;

3) to help in measuring the health related fitness of

the population.

In order to realise these aims, a series of European research seminars on testing physical fitness was organised under the aegis of the Committee for the Development of Sport (Adam et al 1988). Based on the five seminars that took place from 1978 to 1986 the idea for Eurofit was initiated, developed and finalised.

Eurofit, is designed to encompass all areas of physical fitness and includes tests relating to the agility (10 x 5 metres shuttle run), power (standing broad jump), cardio-respiratory endurance (PWC_{170}, cycle ergometer test or 20 metre endurance shuttle run), strength (hand grip), muscular endurance (bent arm hang and sit-ups), body composition (skinfolds), flexibility (sit and reach), speed (plate tapping), and balance (flamingo balance test).

When carrying out a complete Eurofit test the sequence order for testing should be;

1) Flamingo balance test.
2) Plate tapping.
3) Sit and reach.
4) Standing broad jump.
5) Hand grip.
6) Sit-ups.
7) Bent arm hang.

8) 10 x 5 metre shuttle run.

9) Either the 20 metre endurance shuttle run or the PWC_{170} cycle ergometer test.

Skinfolds, height and mass can be recorded at any period during the test.

Before a test was accepted as part of the Eurofit scheme certain criteria needed to be satisfied. Internal (construct) and external (concurrent) validity needed to be acceptable and the reliability and objectivity needed to be high. Also the tests had to be suitable for uses in surveys and large scale projects. Therefore very often simpler versions of the tests were preferred to more sophisticated ones.

Special Note

If the Eurofit tests are to fulfil their purpose then the exercises should not be either learned or practised. Eurofit is designed to be a scientific research tool for assessing a child's fitness and not an exercise regime.

204

References:

Adam C., Klissouras V., Ravazzolo M., Renson R., Tuxworth W. *Handbook for the Eurofit tests of physical fitness*, Council of Europe, Committee for the development of sport, Rome, 1988.

Renson R. Origins, rationale and selection of the Eurofit motor ability tests. *Hermes*, Vol 19, (1), p5-39, 1987-1988.

Tuxworth W., Farrally M.R. Trends and developments in physical education. *Proceedings of the VIII commonwealth and international conference on sport, physical education, dance, recreation and health*, Conference 1986, Glasgow, p18-23, 1986.

TEST 1.   THE FLAMINGO BALANCE TEST

The description and scoring for the flamingo balance test can be found in Chapter 30.

TEST 2.   PLATE TAPPING

Purpose of test: To measure the speed of limb movement.

Equipment: A table with adjustable height, or alternatively a vaulting box as used in a gym. Two rubber discs, 20cm in diameter and a rectangular plate 10 x 20cm. Stopwatch.

Procedure: The two rubber discs centre points are to be placed 80cm apart and horizontally on the table. The rectangular plate should be placed in between the two discs an equal distance from each. Table height should be just below the umbilical level of the subject. With feet slightly apart, the subject places their non-preferred hand on the rectangular plate and the preferred hand over the disc which renders the arms in a crossed fashion. The subject, on the command `ready...start`, should move the preferred hand back and forth between the two discs, (ensuring contact is made with each disc) 50 times for a total of 25 cycles. The stopwatch is started. The stopwatch is stopped when the disc the preferred hand started on is touched for the 25th time. The hand on the rectangular plate stays there during the whole test.

Special notes: The subject may perform a trial to choose the preferred hand. Two attempts are allowed and a rest period is given in between trials, during which time a second subject can perform their first trial. Two testers are recommended: one to time and encourage, the other to count taps. If a subject fails to touch a disc they must perform an extra tap to acheive the 25 cycles required.

Validity and reliability: Acceptable for both or would not be present within Eurofit.

Scoring: The score is the time needed to complete 25 cycles, recorded in tenths of a second.

References: Kemper H.C.C., Dekker H., Ootjers G., Post B., Ritmeester J.W., Snel J., Splinter P., Storm-Van-Essen L., and Verschuur R. *Growth and Health of Teenagers. Appendix.* Repro-Afd Psychologisch Laboratorium, Netherlands, p53-55. 1983.

Ostyn M., Simons J., Beunen G., Renson R., and Van-Gerven. *Aspects of physical fitness of youth-selected topics.* Studiecentrum voor de Fysieke Ontwikkeling bij Jongeren, Leuven, p38, 1980.

Van-Mechelan W., Van-Lier W.H., Hlobiil H., Crolla I., and Kemper H.C.G. Dutch Eurofit Reference Scales for Boys and Girls aged 12-16. In *Pediatric Work Physiology*, Eds. Coudert, J. and Van-Praagh, E. Masson, Paris, Milan, Barcelone and Bonn, p123-125, 1992.

TEST 3.   SIT AND REACH

The description and scoring for the sit and reach test can be found in Chapter 6.

TEST 4. STANDING BROAD JUMP

The description and scoring for the standing broad jump can be found in Chapter 13.

TEST 5.   HANDGRIP

The description and scoring for the handgrip test can be found in Chapter 7.

TEST 6.   SIT-UPS

The description of the procedure for sit-ups can be found in Chapter 20. The scoring for the sit-up test in Eurofit is slightly different however. Instead of recording the number of sit-ups in 60 seconds, the score is the number of sit-ups recorded in 30 seconds.

TEST 7.   BENT ARM HANG

The procedure is very similar to that of the flexed arm hang found in Chapter 22. Slight amendments need to be implemented to bring it exactly into line with the Eurofit method.

1)   A bar diameter of 2.5cm should be used.

2)   The test ends when the subjects eyes fall below the level of bar,

rather than when the subject's chin falls below the level of the bar.

3) The score is the time recorded in tenths of a second rather than seconds.

TEST 8.   **10 x 5 METRE SHUTTLE RUN**

Purpose of test: To test running speed and agility.

Equipment: A clean slip-proof floor. Measuring tape, self adhesive tape or chalk, four traffic cones or similar markers and a stopwatch.

Procedure: A rectangle 5m by 1.2m is marked out with either the chalk or the adhesive tape. A cone or marker is placed at each of the four corners of the rectangle. The subject stands behind one of the 1.2m lines. When the start signal is given the subject runs as fast as possible to the other line and then returns to the starting line, ensuring both feet completely cross both lines. This is 1 cycle and must be repeated 5 times. On the last 5m stretch no turn is required and the subject is encouraged to run as fast as possible over it. The watch is stopped when one of the subjects feet completely crosses the finish line.

Special notes: The test is only performed once. The subject should not slip and slide during the test so a slip-proof floor is essential.

Validity and reliability: Acceptable for both or would not be within Eurofit.

Scoring: The time required to complete 5 cycles is recorded in tenths of a second.

References: Kemper H.C.G., Verschuur R., de Mey L., Storm-Van-Essen L., Van-Zundert A. Longitudidal change in physical fitness of males and females from age 12 to 23. The Amsterdam growth and health study. *Hermes*, Vol 21, (2/3), p-299-314, 1990.

Kemper H.C.C., Dekker H., Ootjers G., Post B., Ritmeester J.W., Snel J., Splinter Storm-Van-Essen L., and Verschuur R. *Growth and Health of Teenagers*. Appendix. Repro-Afd Psychlogisch Laboratorium, Netherlands, p53-55, 1983.

Ostyn M., Simons J., Beunen G., Renson R., and Van-Gerven D. *Aspects of the Physical Fitness of Youth-Selected Topics*. Studiecentrum voor de Fysieke Ontwikkeling bij Jongeren, Leuven, p38, 1980.

Van Mechelen W., Van Lier W.H., Hlobil H., CrollaI and Kemper H.C.G. *World-Wide Variation in Physical Fitness*. Institute of Physical Education, p182-186, 1986.

TEST 9. **PWC$_{170}$.**

The description and scoring for the PWC$_{170}$ test can be found in Chapter 16.

TEST 10. 20m SHUTTLE RUN

The description and scoring for the 20 metre shuttle run test can be found in Chapter 17.

TEST 11. **ANTHROPOMETRIC MEASUREMENTS**

Height: Measured using either an anthropometer or stadiometer. The subject stands straight against an upright surface, with their heels, buttocks and back touching it. With heels together a deep breath is taken and held while height is measured to the nearest millimetre.

Weight: A beam balance or spring balance (provided its accuracy has been recently checked) should be used. Wearing the minimum of clothing the subject stands on the middle of the scales and mass is recorded to the nearest tenth of a kilogram.

Skinfolds: The procedure and method for skinfold measurement has been described in Chapter 26, where the AAHPER Health Related Fitness Test is described. Some slight amendments however, do need to be implemented and a further 3 skinfold sites need to be described.

Equipment: The Harpenden skinfold calipers need only be used for research purposes (ie in the establishment of reference norms). Cheaper plastic calipers (if validated against more accurate makes) may be used by the general practitioner.

Procedure: The triceps and subscapular sites are located and measured as described in Chapter 26.

The biceps skinfold is found in front of the arm, directly above the centre of the cubital fossa. The fold is picked up at the front of the arm, level halfway on a line connecting the acromion and the olecranon processes.

The anterior suprailliac skinfold is picked up 5-7cm above the anterior superior illiac spine on a line to the anterior axillary border, and on a diagonal line going downwards and inwards at 45 degrees.

The medial calf skinfold is picked up on the leg, at the level of the maximum girth of the calf. This is the only skinfold measurement taken with the subject in the seated position.

Scoring: Scoring is taken to the nearest 0.1 mm.

Figure 27.1: Belgium and Dutch data for
the 10 x 5 metre shuttle run.

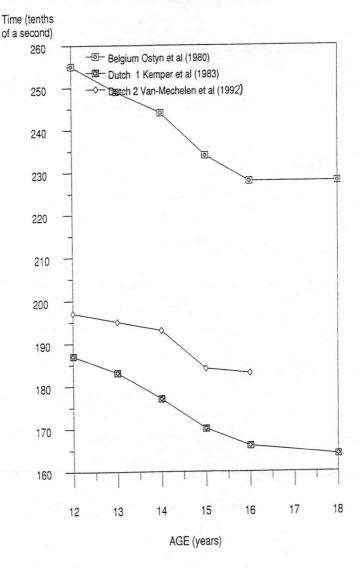

Figure 27.2: Dutch data for girls performing the 10 x 5 metre shuttle run.

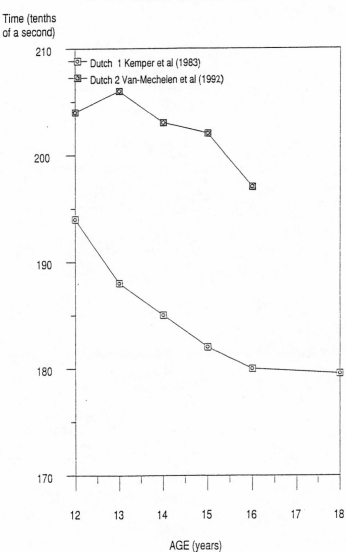

Time (tenths of a second)

AGE (years)

Figure 27.3: Dutch data for boys plate tapping

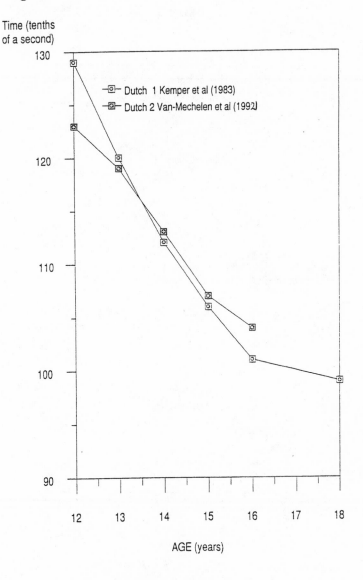

Figure 27.4: Dutch data for girls plate tapping

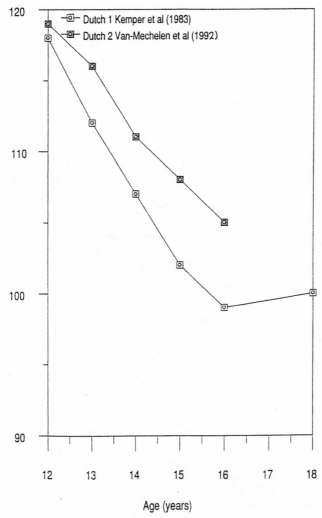

Age (years)

CHAPTER 28 : FORCED VITAL CAPACITY (FVC).

Purpose of test: It provides an estimation of the size of the lungs. Residual volume is not included and therefore it is not a complete measure of the entire lung.

Common usages: Mostly administered in fitness and/or health clinics to assess the effects of disease, smoking and the environment.

Equipment: A single - breath dry spirometer, (eg Vitalograph) is commonly used.

Procedure: The spirometer is calibrated before the measurement is taken. Whilst standing/sitting the individual exhales as fast and as deeply as possible, into a tube which is connected to the spirometer. Individuals exhale for a period of between 4-6 seconds depending on the type of spirometer. It is important that the individual wears a nose clip to ensure that no air escapes through the nose. The spirometer will typically produce a printout in the form of a graph.

The test should be performed a number of times for familiarity and the best test score should be taken.

Special notes: The only air that remains in the lung is termed the residual volume. It averages between 1.0 -1.2 litres for women and 1.2-1.4 litres for men. Lung volume varies with age, gender and body size, especially stature. Lung volume therefore should only be evaluated in relation to norms based on age, gender and size. When administering the test technicians should offer verbal encouragement.

Validity and reliability: Reliability $r=0.8$, $p<0.01$.

Scoring: Forced vital capacity is the maximum amount of air exhaled during the test and therefore is equal to the peak value taken from the Vitalograph or other recording method.

References: Adams G.M. *Exercise Physiology Laboratory Manual*. Wm C. Brown Publishers, Dubuque, 149-157, 1990.

American Thoracic Society. Lung fuction testing: selection of reference values and interpretative strategies. *American Review of Respiratory Diseases*, 1441, 1202-1218, 1991.

Crapo R., Morris A.H., Gardner R.M. Reference spirometric values using techniques and equipment that meet ATS recommendations. *American Review of Respiratory Disease*, 123, 659-664, 1981.

Hibbert M.E., Lannigen A., Landau L. and Phelan P.D. Lung fuction values from longitudinal study of healthy children and adolescents. *Paediatric Pulmonology*, 7, 101-109, 1989.

Miller J.G., Saunders M.J., Gilson R.J.C., Ashcroft M.T. Lung function of healthy boys and girls in Jamaica. *Thorax*, 32, 490, 1977.

McArdle W.D., Katch F.I. and Katch V. *Exercise Physiology: Energy, Nutrition and Human Performance*. Lea and Febiger, Philadelphia, 1991.

Morris J.F., Koski A., Johnson L.C. Spirometric standards for heathly non-smoking adults. *American Review of Respiratory Disease*, 103, 64, 1971.

TABLE 28.1: Predicted forced vital capacity values for males and females.

HEIGHT (cm)	AGE (yr)	MALE FVC (litres)	FEMALE FVC (litres)
155	20	4.22	3.59
	30	4.01	3.37
	40	3.79	3.16
	50	3.58	2.94
	60	3.37	2.72
	70	3.15	2.51
160	20	4.52	3.83
	30	4.31	3.62
	40	4.09	3.40
	50	3.88	3.19
	60	3.67	2.97
	70	3.45	2.75
165	20	4.82	4.08
	30	4.61	3.86
	40	2.39	3.65
	50	4.18	3.43
	60	3.97	3.22
	70	3.75	3.00
170	20	5.12	4.32
	30	4.95	4.11
	40	4.69	3.89
	50	4.48	3.68
	60	4.27	3.46
	70	4.05	3.24
175	20	5.42	4.57
	30	5.21	4.35
	40	4.99	4.14
	50	4.78	3.92
	60	4.57	3.71
	70	4.35	3.49
180	20	5.72	4.82
	30	5.51	4.60
	40	5.29	4.38
	50	5.08	4.17
	60	4.87	3.95
	70	4.65	3.74
185	20	6.02	
	30	5.81	
	40	5.59	
	50	5.38	
	60	5.17	
	70	4.95	

Modified from Crapo R. , Morris A.H , Gardner R.M (1981).

Figure 28.1: Normal forced vital capacity values for males and females (Morris et al 1971)

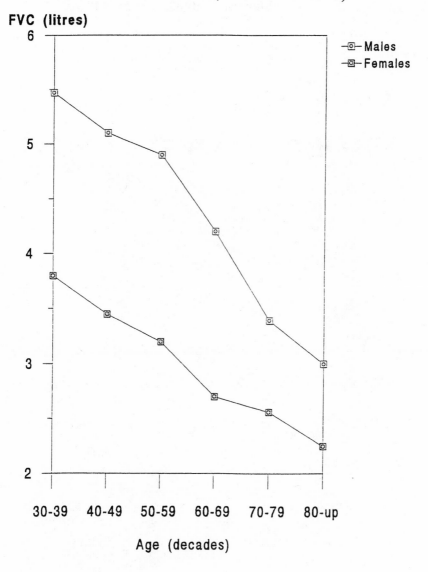

FVC (litres)

Age (decades)

Figure 28.2: Ethnic differences in forced vital capacity for ten year old males and females (Miller et al 1977)

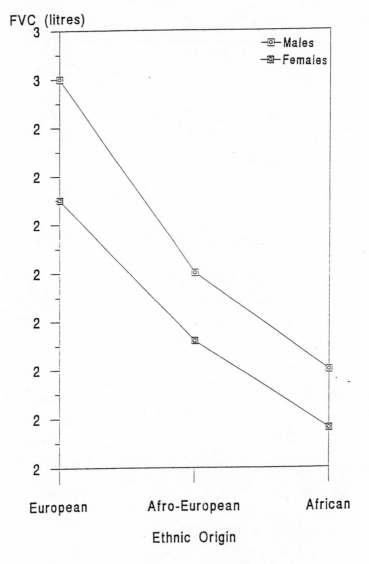

CHAPTER 29 : FORCED EXPIRATORY VOLUME IN ONE SECOND (FEV$_1$).

Purpose of test: Provides an indication of expiratory power and overall resistance to air movement in the lungs.

Common usage: A measurement used to detect obstructive lung disease.

Equipment: A spirometer is used. Results are recorded as with FVC.

Procedure: The spirometer is calibrated before the measurement is taken. Whilst standing/sitting the individual exhales into a tube which is connected to the spirometer. It is important that the individual exhales with as much force and as quickly as possible for the measurement to be accurate. Individuals exhale for a period of between 4-6 seconds depending on the type of spirometer. A nose clip is worn to ensure that no air escapes from the nose during the test. A printout in the form of a a graph is produced.

Special notes: Normally about 85% of the vital capacity can be expelled in one second. The demarcation point for airway obstruction is commonly the point at which less than 70% of the vital capacity can be expired in one second.

Validity and reliability: Reliability $r=0.8$, $p<0.01$

Scoring: The score of the individual's forced expiratory volume is determined by reading the value in litres at one second.

TABLE 29.1 Predicted forced expiratory volume in one second values for males and females.

HEIGHT(cm)	AGE (yr)	MALE FEV_1 (litres)	FEMALE FEV_1 (litres)
155	20	3.74	3.21
	30	3.49	2.96
	40	3.25	2.70
	50	3.01	2.45
	60	2.76	2.19
	70	2.52	1.94
160	20	3.95	3.38
	30	3.70	3.13
	40	3.46	2.87
	50	3.21	2.62
	60	2.97	2.36
	70	2.73	2.11
165	20	4.15	3.55
	30	3.91	3.30
	40	3.66	3.05
	50	3.42	2.79
	60	3.18	2.53
	70	2.93	2.28
170	20	4.36	3.73
	30	4.12	3.47
	40	3.87	3.22
	50	3.63	2.96
	60	3.38	2.71
	70	3.14	2.45
175	20	4.57	3.90
	30	4.32	3.64
	40	4.08	3.39
	50	3.84	3.13
	60	3.59	2.88
	70	3.35	2.62
180	20	4.77	4.07
	30	4.53	3.81
	40	4.29	3.56
	50	4.04	3.30
	60	3.80	3.05
	70	3.55	2.79
185	20	4.98	
	30	4.74	
	40	4.49	
	50	4.25	
	60	4.01	
	70	3.76	

Modified from Crapo R , Morris A.H , Gardner R.M (1981)

226

References:

Adams G.M. *Exercise Physiology Laboratory Manual*. Wm C. Brown Publishers, Dubuque, 149-157, 1990.

American Thoracic Society. Lung fuction testing: Selection of reference values and interpretative strategies. *American Review of Respiratory Diseases*, 1441, 1202-1218, 1991.

Crapo R., Morris A.H., Gardner R.M. Reference spirometric values using techniques and equipment that meet ATS recommendations. *American Review of Respiratory Disease*, 123, 659-664, 1981.

Hibbert M.E., Lannigen A., Landau L. and Phelan P.D. Lung fuction values from longitudinal study of healthy children and adolescents. *Paediatric Pulmonology*, 7, 101-109, 1989.

Miller J.G., Saunders M.J., Gilson R.J.C., Ashcroft M.T. Lung function of healthy boys and girls in Jamaica. *Thorax*, 32, 490, 1977.

McArdle W.D., Katch F.I. and Katch V. *Exercise Physiology: Energy, Nutrition and Human Performance*. Lea and Febiger, Philadelphia, 1991.

Morris J.F., Koski A., Johnson L.C. Spirometric

standards for healthy non-smoking adults. *American Review of Respiratory Disease*, 103, 64, 1971.

Figure 29.1: Normal forced expiratory volume in one second values for males and females (Morris et al, 1971)

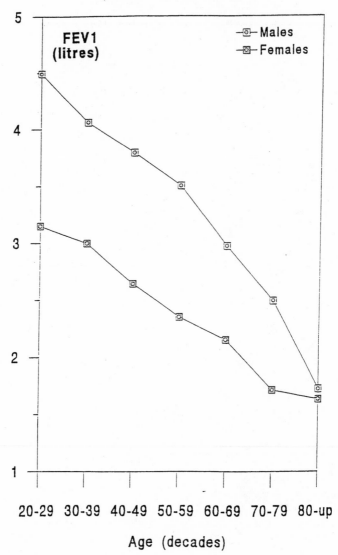

Figure 29.2: Ethnic differences in forced expiratory volume in one second for ten year old males and females (Miller et al, 1977)

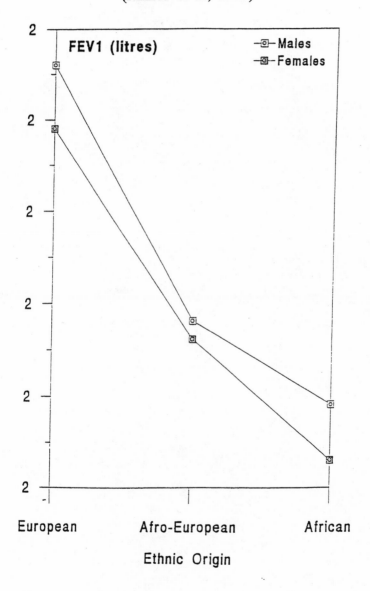

FEV1 (litres)

-◙- Males
-◙- Females

European   Afro-European   African

Ethnic Origin

CHAPTER 30 : STORK STAND STATIC BALANCE TEST

Purpose of test: To assess the ability of the motor system to maintain equilibrium in a stationary position.

Common usages: Has been used to assess the balancing ability of dancers (Shick et al, 1983). It is most commonly used for college age students of either sex.

Equipment: A smooth flat non-slip surface is required. Stopwatch.

Procedure: The subject stands on the preferred leg, and places the sole of the other foot against the inside of the knee of the supporting leg. The hands are placed on the hips. On command of the tester, the subject raises the heel of the supporting foot off the ground and attempts to maintain balance for as long as possible.

Special Notes: Little data are available for young and elderly populations. A more common procedure for these groups is the Single Leg Stance Stand. This is essentially the same as the Stork Test except the heel is left in contact with the ground. For children it is suggested that a visual focus point is also used (Atwater et al, 1990). Elderly subjects who have a history of falling during gait have been found to displace their mass more to the side during this test (Crosbie et al, 1989). For young and elderly subjects, a "spotter" (to prevent falling) should be used. Patla et al (1990) states that static balance tests are not valid for the assessment of balance during gait.

Validity and Reliability: Face validity for both the Stork Stand and the Single Leg Stance Stand is accepted.

Reliability of between $r=0.87$ to $r=0.99$ has been reported for the Single Leg Stand (Atwater et al, 1990) and $r=0.82$ (Shick et al, 1983). Reliability for the Stork Stand was found to be $r=0.79$.

Scoring: The score is the maximum number of seconds between the heel being raised and balance being lost. Three trials are performed with the highest score recorded.

Limitations: For pathological populations this test fails to give sufficient information. For further reading refer to

Duncan (1989) and Newton (1989).

An alternative to the Stork Stand is the **Flamingo Balance Test**, which is cited as part of the Eurofit test battery (1988).

Purpose: To assess general balance ability.

Common usages: Designed to be used with children of school-age.

Equipment: Metal beam; length 50 cm, height 4 cm and width 3 cm, covered with material (maximum depth 5 mm). The beam is stabilised by two supports, length 15 cm, width 2 cm. Stopwatch.

Procedure: The subject stands on the long axis of the beam using the preferred foot. The knee of the non-weighted leg is fully flexed and the foot is placed behind the pelvis. The foot is grasped by the hand on the same side, and the other arm is used for balancing. The test and the stopwatch is stopped when the free leg is released, or when any part of the body touches the floor. After each loss of balance the test is recommenced and timing resumed until 60 seconds elapses.

Validity and Reliability: Face validity is assumed. Reliability is not known.

Special notes: If the subject falls 15 times within the first 30 seconds, the test is stopped, and the subject is recorded as not having completed the test. This may occur in the 6-9 year age group.

Scoring: The number of attempts (not falls) required to remain in balance on the beam for 60 seconds.

Limitations: This test appears to be described solely in Eurofit (1988) and as such, no comparable data is available. However, subjectively, fewer balance attempts required represent superior balancing performance. This test is therefore useful as a screening test suitable for school assessments.

References: Atwater S.W., Crowe T.K., Deitz J.C. and Richardson P. Inter-rater and test-retest reliability of two pediatric balance Tests. *Physical Therapy*, 70, (2) 79-87, 1990.

Crosbie W.J., Nimmo N.A., Banks M.A., Brownlee M.G. and Meldrum F. Standing balance responses in two populations of elderly women: a pilot study. *Archives of Physical Medicine and Rehabilitation*, 70, (10) 751-754, 1989.

Duncan P.W., Studentski S. Chandler J., Bloomfeld R. and La Pointe L. Electromyographic analysis of postural adjustments in two methods of balance testing. *Physical Therapy,* 70, 88-96, 1989.

Eurofit. European test of physical fitness. *Council of Europe. Committee for the development of sport.* Rome, 42-43, 1988.

Iverson B.D., Gossman M.R., Shaddeau S.A. and Turner M.E. Balance performance, force production and activity levels in non-institutionalised men aged 60-90 years. *Physical Therapy,* 70,(6), 348-355, 1990.

Newton R. Review of tests of standing balance abilities *Brain Injury,* 3,(4), 335-343, 1989.

Patla A., Frank J. and Winter D. Assessment of balance control in the elderly: major issues. *Physiotherapy Canada,* 42,(2), 89-97, 1990.

Shick J., Stoner L.J. and Jette N. Relationship between modern-dance experience and balancing performance. *Research Quarterly For Exercise And Sport,* 54,(1), 79-82, 1983.

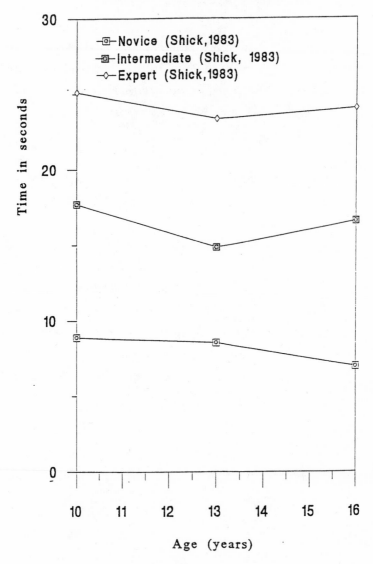

Figure 30.1: Stork stand balance times for dancers of differing experience

Figure 30.2: Graph showing single leg support balance times for children

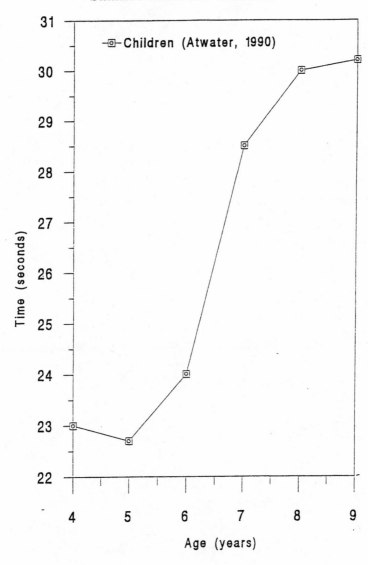

Figure 30.3: Graph showing single leg support balance times for elderly men.

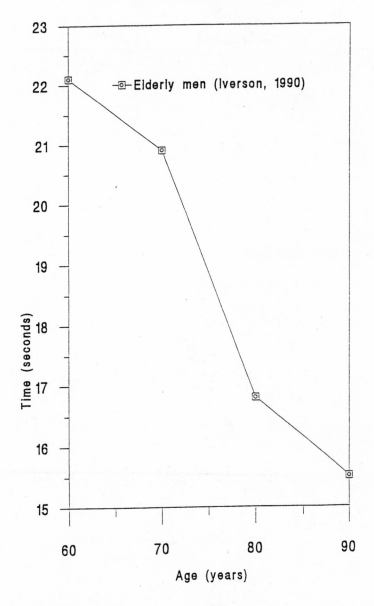